I0521660

The Boss Up Effect

The Official Black Millennial Guide to Increasing Your Income & Taking Control of Your Career

By

Kaila B. Epps

Black Excellence Publishing

First published in the United States of America.

All rights reserved. Except for brief quotations in a review, no part of this book may be reproduced or transmitted, in any form or by any means, electronic or mechanical (including photocopying), nor may it be stored in any information storage and retrieval system without written permission from the publisher.

DISCLAIMER

The advice contained in this material might not be suitable for everyone. The author designed the information to present her opinion about the subject matter. The reader must carefully investigate all aspects of any business decision before committing him or herself. The author obtained the information contained herein from sources she believes to be reliable and from her personal experience, but she neither implies nor intends any guarantee of accuracy. The author is not in the business of giving legal, accounting, or professional advice. Should the reader need such advice, he or she must seek services from a competent professional. The author particularly disclaims any liability, loss, or risk taken by individuals who directly or indirectly act on the information contained herein. The author believes the advice presented here is sound. Still, readers cannot hold her responsible for either their actions or the risk taken by individuals who directly or indirectly act on the information contained herein.

Published by Black Excellence Publishing
A division of The Recruit Refinery LLC
Printed in the United States
Design by Murad
Copyright © 2022 by Kaila B. Epps, MBA, CPC
ISBN 979-8-9852050-3-9

Acknowledgments

To Father God, Yeshua, and Mother Wisdom for guidance, clarity, intuition, and a renewed mind to help others and grow within my own journey. To Mikayah for pushing me out of my comfort zone and encouraging me to follow my passions, even when I fussed. Your support has been unwavering, and you have helped shape me into the woman I am today. To my sister Stephanie for connecting me with the roles that helped transform my life and always supporting my journey and pouring into me. To my mother, Tracey, for your support and instilling the importance of educating and bettering myself. To my clients who helped refine my craft and taught me so much along the way. Your success inspires me. And to my support group of peers, mentors, and family that encourage and help remind me of my why. Thank you.

Table of Contents

INTRODUCTION

Hi, family of Black excellence! My name is Kaila Epps - a certified professional coach with an MBA in General Management and career experience as an HR business partner. This book aims to help Black millennials propel their careers and increase their earning potential by building confidence in their professional and networking skills.

I know you may be feeling like you've hit a glass ceiling in your career, possibly feeling undervalued by your manager, or like you've hit a roadblock in your job. Maybe you're struggling to figure out that next move and how to even get started on the process of moving forward.

I've experienced all of these during my career in nonprofit and corporate America, as well as throughout my entrepreneurial journey. Specifically, I've had three big moments in my 9-5 career where I've felt this way, and I'll give you a summary below before going into the steps I implemented to overcome these pivotal moments that propelled me to a 6-figure career.

I attended Spelman College (the #1 HBCU in the nation!) for my undergrad as a Spanish Premed student with hopes of helping Black and Brown communities that weren't properly treated and also as a pediatric cardiovascular surgeon to solve issues of babies born with heart problems. Like most people who go to school, I initially thought I had my whole life figured out. Then I wavered on this path, even though it was what I had planned to do with my life since I could remember. My motto was doctor by day, chef by night, and actress all around. But as I studied abroad in Argentina my junior year and had yet to start preparing for the MCAT, a friend suggested I do a gap year to figure things out.

At this point, taking a gap year felt like failing because I was disrupting what I thought would be the next 15 or so years of my life (med-school, fellowships, rotations in pediatrics and surgical, etc., to opening my own practice eventually). It was a fearful thought, but since I felt my heart wasn't 100% in medicine anymore, I decided to try the gap year after graduating.

My first job out of college was as a math tutor fellow (which was more like a full-blown Algebra teacher) for high school students on the south side of Chicago. I was making a $17,000 salary instead of a stipend like we were initially told (the difference being our salary was *taxed*, so I was actually making *LESS* than that for the *WHOLE YEAR*) living in Hyde Park, of all places, while it was undergoing the wild gentrification that has taken place since (there was still a Radio Shack on the strip on 53rd although they were going out of business). We were making so little money at my job that we didn't qualify for food stamps (which - is that even legal??), and I had to get a side job as a waitress at an Italian restaurant to make ends meet.

During our first month of training in my new role, Mike Brown was murdered, and I asked our Program Director to acknowledge it and have a session to make sure that certain staff understood the cultural differences and socioeconomic traumas that came from the neighborhoods we would be teaching in (which were Black and brown). We had people of all backgrounds as tutors (a good portion of whom had a "captain save-a-child" mentality), and they needed to know how to support our students who faced similar situations of police brutality, racial profiling, etc., in their own lives.

However, I was told that we were just there to teach Algebra, nothing more, nothing less. If our Black (and brown) students were accosted by the police or lost a friend the night before, it didn't matter because all we were to focus on was math, not their mental and emotional well-being. That was the first inkling that I wouldn't stay with the company past that first year because I still wanted to uphold my commitment to the students at my school.

Even with that being said, I still focused a decent portion of my energy on bringing in guests or finding programs to help my students develop personally and professionally outside of "math" class. This was when I realized that I didn't need to go into medicine to directly impact people's lives. It's also where I found my passion for helping others develop. Yet, things would happen time and time again in the program that showed me that they didn't care about my students or me, so it felt like I was in a rut.

I ended up reaching out to a few people in my network, and it was a conversation with my sister that ultimately changed the trajectory of my career path. She got me in contact with the Chicago office of the nonprofit she worked for, where they trained young professionals on business etiquette/professional skills and helped with college access. It was perfect as someone who newly realized my love for the development of self and others. Long story short, I interviewed and got the role, *doubling* my salary within a couple of months of having that conversation with my sister.

So, this job is where the second instance of me feeling like I hit a glass ceiling in my career occurred. Even though I loved the mission and impact we were making at this organization, I again felt like I was in a rut when I asked for further development so I could be in a better position for a promotion. My manager told me that they didn't know how to develop me. And then, shortly after that, the directors pulled us into a staff meeting to walk through the five-year plan. The only new jobs that were being added were about three on my current level, one managerial position that had just been filled, and an extra director-level position. When I asked about instating other roles, like having an actual HR role (which had similarities to the one I was in), I was told it wasn't in the cards. I once again felt like I was stuck, hitting a brick wall.

I happened to let my mentor know what was happening (I met him because he volunteered for a financial literacy workshop we were hosting for our students), and we discussed other options, including going to business school. From there, we worked on my applications, I attended a plethora of events, and got into a top 20 program on a full ride!

This then brings us to the third instance of feeling undervalued and like I needed to make a change. It came from the full-time position I accepted once I graduated from my MBA program, and it was the icing on the cake of being undervalued and being in an environment that wasn't conducive to my health or education. I was staffing $2MM+ projects, sitting at the table with managers and coaching them through performance management and hiring strategies, training others and creating development programs for them. Still, I wasn't getting any development for myself... once again. I don't fault my manager 100% for this because this person was thrown into the fire and wasn't getting the proper support they needed either. On top of that, a couple of people on my team had been there for *years* without the slightest inkling of a promotion coming their way. They were told that they couldn't promote due to organizational structure or that they didn't have the "education" for promotion even though they had more experience at the site than most folks on my team combined, *including* my manager... Shame.

I was tired of hitting these brick walls and being at companies that didn't care enough to invest in my development. I decided to step out on my own as a career coach because I wanted to help others who also kept facing these situations. I've seen that for every deserving person who is being stunted in their career, there is someone less capable in comparison being promoted or rewarded in their stead. And there had to be a reason.

So, I wrote this to give people access to the information that seemed to be only known to a minority—unwritten rules of the workplace. How having family, friends, or other connections in places can be the ultimate reason you get the job over someone else, even if you are not "qualified" for the roles. How being able to "sell" yourself is highly important and can get you to where you want to be in your career.

Even though it's true for all parties, I saw time and time again that Black employees were the ones who tended not to get the development needed, not have the connections that could help them, or not have the skills to sell their value to a manager. I looked back on my own experience, the things that I did to pivot, and what I could do to help others.

In each of these instances, I knew that getting guidance, whether through coaching, reading books, etc., would help me figure it out. Each time I wasn't getting what I needed, I took it upon myself to get my own development and utilized my mentors and network along the way. I implemented the strategies laid out in this book and propelled myself forward, and, in turn, propelled my income to levels I never even thought possible.

Through drawing upon my work experiences, gaining my coaching certifications, and connecting with other like-minded individuals, I was able to break free from that ceiling and forge a career path that involves doing what I love - empowering others to develop personally and professionally!

Through that, I've been able to help other business owners and working professionals move forward in their careers through gaining employment, pivoting in their businesses, booking speaking engagements, and gaining confidence in their value and abilities to do what they put their minds to.

This is why I'm passionate about helping professionals like yourself level up in their careers and increase their opportunities for higher income. I'd seen the people around me in every role I've held be undervalued and held back, and I'd experienced it too many times for my liking. And I decided it was time for a change.

People say that the process of finding a career that you're passionate about is more of a pipedream than a reality. They also say that the recruiting process is daunting and uptight. But the truth is - the process of figuring out who you are and what you enjoy is well worth your time! *Then* finding companies that align with those values or a line of work that serves you can be just as fun and very rewarding.

Just during the pandemic alone, 4.4 million new businesses were started, and workers around the globe took back their voices on what they wanted from their companies (work-life balance, DEI, benefits, etc.). In fact, people have started taking so much ownership over their careers and lives to have the work lifestyle they want, that it's being called "The Great Resignation" - where employees began resigning from their jobs en masse beginning in late 2020. Apparently, a whopping 75.4 million people left their jobs by September of 2021 to find careers that were more fulfilling! This information alone should be enough to light a fire under you to take control of your career! You are not alone. You can do this!

Thus, my solution for you is to follow the steps outlined in this book to help you gain clarity in your career and take the steps that will help you lead the life you want. And you will be more confident on the other side than when you started this thing.

During my journey, the one mistake that would give me pause or that I saw that held people back was mindset. Not having the proper mindset keeps people in a state of "stuck" and believing that they can't have more for themselves - financially or professionally.

Therefore, we'll discuss this in the first chapter to ensure that you surpass this one thing that could hold you back from taking action for the rest of the journey.

The good news is that you bought this book already, which says you are on the right path with your mindset, and puts you light years ahead of others just wishing something "would change." You are here to make that change, and for that, I say congratulations!

CHAPTER 1

Refine Your Mind (Mind Over Matter)

If you watch most interviews with successful people or multimillionaires, nine times out of ten, they'll mention that they've read or listened to "Think and Grow Rich." The book discusses having a mindset shift and utilizing desire through autosuggestion to manifest what you want.

Although I hadn't heard of nor read this book until more recently, during those times when I was hitting those roadblocks in my career, I had some similarities in my mindset of attracting what I knew I wanted. I put my energy into where I wanted my life to go, not into what I *didn't* want or the *negative* feelings I was having. Those things became minuscule in the grand scheme of things.

An example of this came from when I was still in my first role out of school. I was feeling miserable and wrote a letter to my best friend (yes, I said a letter - I'm quite old school that way) and told them that I wanted to make 3x more than what I was making at the time, which would be about $51,000. That was my goal—just an extra $34k per year.

The first step was that my mindset shifted. I was in such a terrible place mentally and emotionally working at my job. A lot of times, I had no idea what my future would hold. However, I decided that I had enough and was worth more than what I was being paid at the time. I knew I wanted better for myself, so I wrote that I would make it happen.

I opened my mind to the possibility of having more. I looked past my current situation and began envisioning a future where I was making a greater impact and more money. This was the beginning phase of attracting the things that I wanted. So with that mindset, I doubled my income in less than a year after writing that letter. And overall, I ended up over 5x'ing that original amount I was making.

It was vital to change how I thought about myself, my circumstances, and even the people in my life. There was a shift that was taking place inside of me. I was fed up, but I didn't stay stagnant like many people around me. I had shifted my mind from being in a state of complacency to wanting more and being willing to do whatever (ethically) to make it happen. I didn't fall into a negative pattern of complaining without bringing solutions. I may have started off there, but after being mistreated and seeing others also get caught in the crossfire, I knew that wasn't the way for me to get out of my situation.

Initially, fear kept me stagnant in a job I hated. We all have it. It just may show itself in different ways. For me, I had a fear of success, not necessarily a fear of failure. In my eyes, failure was to be expected when it came to dreaming big or wanting more than average for myself. This was because of the multiple disappointments I had experienced in my personal life and witnessing people from the environment I grew up in, even though many of my friends and family would describe me as "successful."

Upon reflection, I had dispelled this fear multiple times because I was a first-generation college student. I was the first person in my family to attend and graduate from an HBCU and full-time graduate program. And I've traveled to 21 countries around the world and worked my way up to making six figures from a $17,000 salary after leaving college. All of these things can be considered more than average - but to me, this was what I was *supposed* to be doing. It wasn't *above* average, like owning real estate or being a millionaire. It wasn't above average like owning and running my own businesses. There were no examples of this in my family for real.

So I decided that I didn't like how I was feeling or the effect it was having on my personal and professional relationships or work ethic. I began a journey to create that mental shift within myself to believe that I was more than capable. At the end of the day, only I truly had power and control over my thoughts and mind. And once I came to that revelation, I decided what things I wanted to put into my mind and my thoughts daily. I decided what type of messaging I wanted to tell myself; messaging which was no longer negative things but more affirming and positive messaging to help me get to a level of mental health that would allow me to reach the goals I truly wanted and desired. I then took action based on the positive results that I wanted.

More recently, while reapplying these concepts, I was able to write this book and pursue other business opportunities that

I view as successful. I have branched out in my network of people who can help me succeed in the things I truly desire. I no longer hold myself back. I am going after what I desire and am passionate about, and I am in a space to help others do the same.

And I'm excited to do so!

So all of that to say: only you have power and control over your mind. What you feed it, whether positive or negative, will influence your actions at some point, and it can contribute to your success, or it can contribute to your shortcomings. Therefore, to start on a path to fulfill your goals and dreams, you will need to refine your mind.

So now you might be asking: "How do I change my mindset?" or "That sounds great, Kaila, but I don't know how to make that happen." Or you could even be thinking, "What does that have to do with me taking control of my career?"

That is why I'm *emphasizing* the importance of this chapter. Because before you can do anything else in your journey, it is vital to get your mind right in order for you to be successful in every aspect of your life. You have to change your mindset if you want to change your world and your circumstances.

So to your question of "How do I change my mindset?" my answer is this:

First - You need to leave behind the spirit of fear because all it'll do is hold you back, make you doubt yourself, and keep you stuck exactly where you are, which I'm pretty sure is exactly what you *don't* want.

For example, if you've ever come up with an idea or made some type of plan to do something, but then started going through *all* the different thoughts and reasons of why it will fail and how it can fail or the reasons why you're not qualified enough or nobody's going to believe in you, that is the spirit of fear taking over.

In the world of coaching, we call it "limiting beliefs."

And this is nothing to be ashamed of. We all have suffered from it at some point, if not currently. We live in a society where it's always trying to instill fear into us, whether through news reports, TV ads and commercials, or even through our education system or religious institutions.

There are always some elements of fear involved. This is why you must control the type of media you intake and the group of people you hang around. If you're surrounded by negativity all the time, then all you will think are negative thoughts, and in turn, you'll feel negative and react negatively to your circumstances. You'll likely be less inclined to start taking actions that can help your situation.

This fear holds us hostage to staying in jobs that we know are not good for us. It holds us hostage to staying in relationships we know are toxic. It makes us risk-averse; therefore, we don't take a chance on ourselves with something that could help us succeed and set us financially free.

That is how it relates to your professional life *and* personal life. *That* is how it has to do with this book which is about helping *you* to boss up and take control of a career path you love with confidence. Now, this isn't to say you won't have a feeling of fear or get scared or nervous about things. That's completely natural. But to stay in a constant, perpetual state of fearing things and allowing that to dictate how you operate and move is completely different and deeper.

You *have* to combat this spirit if you want to move forward. "For God hath not given us the spirit of fear: but of power, and love, and of a sound mind." - 2 Timothy 1:7 KJV.

Even if you aren't spiritual or subscribe to a specific religion, this still rings true, given the examples in the previous paragraphs. It rings true if you're regretting past things and have thoughts like, "If I had just taken that chance...."

Again, I can say from experience that this is something I had to battle for a very long time. Know that it doesn't just affect your life professionally. It affects you personally as well. It can dictate your decisions and make you create situations worse for yourself than if you had reacted positively.

As Paulo Coehlo said, "*Tell your heart that the fear of suffering is worse than the suffering itself... and no heart has ever suffered when it's gone in search of its dream...*"

It means that because you don't want to experience whatever horror you've concocted in your mind, you are holding yourself hostage from moving forward. This is sad because the reality is, if you face the situation, you'll see that those negative thoughts in your mind are worse than what will actually transpire. When you realize this, you actually *grow and heal* when you take that step forward versus staying stuck in limbo due to the fear.

But a lot of times, we don't recognize it as fear. We may think it's just our personalities, or that's just how things are, or it could show itself in the form of being controlling.

So to mitigate this behavior for the future, there are a few things that you can do to help set you free from this overwhelming spirit. Once I did this, I began to feel such a difference in my day to day and in my drive to achieve my greatest desires.

They are as follows:

Steps to Overcome the Spirit of Fear:

1. Self-Reflect and Assess

Take a moment to assess why you have these fears or thoughts in your mind. Once you figure that out, it'll help you with the second step of acknowledging and facing the reasons behind it.

Now, depending on the situation and how deep the reasons run, you may need to dig into family history or face some traumas to get to the root of things. For me, it was facing some abandonment issues and realizing how that was affecting not only my life personally, but how it trickled into things I was doing professionally as well. However, for this book, we'll keep it light. I will always advocate therapy in any situation because it makes a world of difference, even if you aren't going through anything "traumatic" presently. You can get helpful exercises and tools to help you move past any mental roadblocks you may be having.

Therapists can help you get to the bottom of those issues if you let them. It takes a village, and there can be someone on your team who holds you accountable, helps you see yourself in a different light, and pushes you toward healthy behaviors and thought patterns. That being said, make sure you find someone who is a fit for you.

Another thing is to reflect on your previous behaviors or experiences to see if outside factors influenced or clouded your judgment and mind, such as alcohol or other vices. We may not realize it, but these things can carry spirits and bring out parts of us that aren't conducive to our growth or may cause unhealthy behaviors and mindsets.

For me, it was alcohol. After some years, I realized that drinking caused me to operate in a lower frequency of myself. I was constantly having an immense rush of negative thoughts and feelings, and reacting in a negative manner towards people and situations that didn't necessarily warrant that big of a response. Once I figured this out and stopped drinking all-together, it was easier for me to focus my mind on positive thoughts to counteract anything negative that kept trying to surface and hold me back taking actions that would help me reach my goals.

It's easy in this step to beat yourself up and start going on a tailspin of regret, but don't do this. You can't change your past actions or mindsets; all you can focus on is now and how you want to be in the future. Make the changes you want to see now; take actions that will move you toward your goals. Take accountability for the things that have happened in the past and just move forward from there. Don't get stuck by continuously reliving situations you can't change and holding on to trauma and fear.

Again, living in a state of trauma is detrimental to your growth. If you were abused, cheated on, treated badly at your job, etc., you *have* to face it in order to move past it. The more you try to bury it or just live in *your* version of the "full reality," it will hinder you and keep you stuck mentally and spiritually.

2. Acknowledge, Face, and Shift

This is probably the hardest step, but it's super important because this is where you start to take accountability and allow yourself some grace and mercy. Take a moment to realize that you are human. A lot of times, the things that we deal with outside carry themselves into the workplace with us, and the habits that we develop start to show themselves and can be damaging.

Once you can acknowledge these thought patterns, certain behaviors, and certain habits, you can start to face them head-on so that you are freeing yourself little by little of whatever mindset got you there. And once you're able to face these issues and acknowledge these thoughts, you'll be able to better shift your mindset into a more positive place and be more pointed in your thoughts.

I'll give a quick example of what this could look like. There have been multiple points in my career where I was going through something personal, and I was checked out at work. I was more irritable. I didn't care to be there. I also started taking sick days or just calling in because I didn't want to waste what energy I had going into a job that also drained me. I became defensive, a habit I formed outside of work to deal with traumas or issues. I became distrustful of my coworkers and would project things onto them. I had my own feelings of not being good enough from the abandonment I mentioned earlier, so

I'd be hesitant to volunteer for projects I was well qualified for because of how negatively I was feeling inside. Sometimes if I were on a project, I'd second guess myself all the time, even when there was no reason to.

As an HR professional, one of the first things we do when we notice a change in someone's behavior or see that their performance is slipping is to check in with them to see if they've had any major life changes. This makes sense since we allow outside factors to influence how we show up at work.

Is there a co-worker or employee you can think of that started coming in late when they were normally always on time? Maybe they began to miss deadlines or didn't put as much effort into a project they normally would have knocked out of the park? Perhaps someone who was usually chatty and bubbly is now withdrawn and more serious.

These are normally indicators that something isn't right and affects them mentally, emotionally, etc. In turn, it affects their work and their career. However, as I began to face some of the things happening outside of work, it became easier to melt that defensive guard while I was at work. I could feel myself wanting to take actions that would help lead me to the next phase in my career.

In the workplace, they say, "Leave your emotions at the door," which we clearly know is not realistic. So evaluate how you show up to work and make a note of where you are operating in fear. Observe those around you and see if you can better understand the folks who may also be operating in their fears, whether it's the person who's quick to cuss somebody out or who doesn't contribute as much to a project.

At the end of the day, it's about understanding that we are all human; none of us are perfect. We all make mistakes, and sometimes we learn lessons the hard way at others' expense and our own. It may not be fair. And it definitely sucks. We all have a history and a background that contributes to our ideologies, actions, and beliefs.

We can't change the past, but we can change the present. We can grow. We can realize that we are more in control of our lives and careers than the world lets on.

3. Affirm and Repeat

The next step is making some type of affirmations or positive goals toward the future for yourself. These affirmations need to be *personal.*

I don't suggest just finding random affirmations online or in little cards, notebooks, or whatever they have out here because they aren't specific to the thoughts that take hold in your mind. They can be good for general pick-me-ups, but for the deep stuff holding you stagnant, you should create your own.

When you were in the reflection/self-assessment stage, you should have come up with certain thoughts or actions that you want to get rid of, and by doing that, you can now make positive statements and affirmations that counteract those negative feelings, those negative thoughts, and those negative beliefs that you have in yourself OR that someone else may have put on you. And read that last part again: **that someone *else* may have put on you.** We allow others to speak death over us and our situations because of *their* disbelief or personal issues that they project onto us as if it's our problems. Undo that. Speak life over yourself and counteract it.

Make sure that these statements are written somewhere that you can see them daily. Whether you put them on sticky notes on your bathroom mirror or post them on the wall in your bedroom or have them on a board in your office space, they should be visible for you to constantly see and constantly remind yourself of how great you are and that you are more than capable.

Repeat those daily as much as you can until you start feeling that shift in your mindset; that positivity will help you go a long way.

Then you'll be able to more naturally affirm yourself and believe in yourself.

You just need to continue to repeat this cycle until you have that self-confidence that you can do whatever it is that you put your mind to. This may take some time, so don't rush the process. Trust the process. Update these statements and affirmations as you start to grow and overcome one area. It'll make a world of difference in how you show up in your personal life and how you show up in your work.

Again, it takes time to do these steps as you're working toward your goals, but this is vital in helping you reach them.

You don't want to speak death over yourself or your situations (especially given what I said about other people already doing it for you). Remember - life and death truly lie in the power of your tongue. You don't want to trap yourself in the mindset that you can't accomplish these "S.M.A.R.T" goals that we'll lay out. Once you start to believe it, you'll be able to see it, and then you'll be able to achieve it.

Your mental health is everything, and if your mind isn't right, nothing else will be right, at least not for long.

We are starting to see this in our culture more now than ever. Examples are Simone Biles pulling out of the finals for the Olympics and Naomi Osaka doing the same for the French Open. These ladies knew the importance of admitting it was time to put their mental state and mindset first because it was truly affecting their careers.

So don't be afraid to speak up and ask for help. Don't be afraid to get an accountability partner such as a coach (like me), a mentor, which we'll discuss later, or any other services that can help you become a better version of yourself.

If you aren't ready for that step, what I've outlined in this book is the baseline of what you can do to help yourself. Once I started applying these strategies to my own life, it has been a game-changer in allowing me to turn my ideas into action.

Once I made this shift, I was able to double my income, go to business school with a non-traditional background for FREE, and over 5x my original salary. I was able to complete this book that I've been sitting on for a long time. I was able to reach out and network better with people that I look up to in the different fields that I was aspiring to be in, and I was taking risks that normally I would have been too fearful to do. I was booking more speaking engagements as a coach and position-ing myself in a financial space and place I truly wanted. It also brought me to a more fruitful place in my relationships, which was a huge goal.

It all started with me shedding this fearful spirit and operating in power, having that sound mind, and coming from a place of love in all I did.

Remember these things:
- Your mind (and body) are more than capable.
- You are worth it.
- "... for as (a man) thinketh in his heart, so is he." Proverbs 23:7 KJV
- If you can conceive it, you can achieve it.

CHAPTER 2

Figuring out that Next Step

We will be doing a lot of reflection as we move through this journey because you always need to check in with yourself to ensure you're doing what is best for you and that it aligns with your values.

We're going to start by taking a moment to think about what your previous experiences have been: whether it was applying to get a new job, networking, asking for a raise, or pitching your idea for a new project.

Take a moment to write down what things went well and what things went wrong or could have some improvements behind them.

Next, I want you to consider the different feelings you have associated with these situations.

Are they negative? Why?

Are they mostly positive? What is the reason behind that?

If we talk about recruiting for a moment, it's commonplace for people to think of it in a very negative light. You have to be all 'suited and booted' to talk to a bunch of strangers about yourself to get a job, and it's just a very nerve-racking process.

But you can change your perspective to:

"Okay, it's not that I have to meet a bunch of randos, but I'm able to meet new people who can help me get to where I want to go. I'm meeting new people that I can learn from and that I can also bring value to."

If you have to travel, you can think of it as being able to explore a new area that you haven't been to before, especially if you're going out of state.

If you have been there, then maybe you can learn new things about that city and experience it in a new light. You can try new restaurants or visit new stores and shops that you haven't visited before. And you can document the process for future references.

When it comes to interviewing or pitching yourself, think about it as you are gifting the world with your talent and what you bring to the table.

You can have a conversation with someone about something you are passionate about. You can also influence them to be passionate about it, believe in your vision enough to help you get to where you want to be, and hire you for the role because they see the value you add. This is because they're getting to know you personally and seeing your personality come out as they connect with you. After all, humans love connection.

So this process doesn't have to be something scary. It truly can be fun and be a game-changer for your career. The worst that can happen is for someone to say no. And that's not the end of the world. It is just an opportunity to learn how you can better present yourself going forward so that you can get what you need.

Are you in the right space?

As you're reflecting, think about if you want to stay in your current industry. You can make a list of the things you love about it, the things you dislike, and if you're willing to work around the things you dislike or if one list outweighs the other.

Then you can answer the questions: "Why do I want to stay in this industry?" or "Why don't I want to stay in this industry?" At the end of the day, you may want to pivot from your function or industry, which is perfectly okay. People do it all the time. Heck - I did it as well! And I will probably do it again.

That's exactly what happened with one of my clients as we worked together and started to talk more about her passions and values in building her personal brand.

She realized that the current business that she was running wasn't where her passion lay, so I was helping her prepare to re-enter the workforce. However once we began this work, she decided to pivot and create a completely new business. It was a freeing moment for her and a game-changer for her career! Now she's happier and is booked out with speaking engagements for the rest of the year. Talk about a shift!

Many people jump functions at a company as they move their way up. I had a coworker who started in marketing and switched to human resources – Diversity & Inclusion. Even most people who go to business school are changing career paths.

So think about your passions. Make a list of them and put them into separate categories. Think about what roles or companies align with those things and if it's realistic for you to pursue them. Also, write out if you are already seeking them. If not, write out why you aren't pursuing these things.

This will help you determine whether you are faking the funk. Faking the funk is when you are living a life or in a career that is not true to who you are. You found yourself there because you were influenced by other people telling you what was best for you, or you were too afraid to live the way you wanted or have the career you wanted.

We have all experienced this at some point, especially if your parents pressured you to go to college and become a doctor, lawyer, or engineer because it's an occupation *they* could be proud of and brag about you doing. But if, in reality, you truly wanted to go into art school, then you're already placed on the road to faking the funk. If you get a corporate job just because that's what society says you should do, not necessarily what you feel like you should do, then you're faking the funk.

A common misconception that's out there is that you can't just make money from something you're passionate about; you need to have a real job. As I alluded to above, how many of us when we were younger wanted to be artists, actresses/actors, dancers, or chefs and our parents said that we need something real to fall back on?

Or who had teachers or coaches who tried to push sports on them because, as Black people, our only apparent options are sports or the streets? And even with sports, you would still need to have a real fallback.

The irony is that there are plenty of people who are making a living and are very well off from those "non-real" jobs. And due to the pandemic, many people decided to take a step back to start pursuing things they were passionate about because they had no other choice BUT to reflect on their lives while sitting at home in lockdown. So many of us are returning to the things that are special to us or that were important to us in our younger years because that is the truth of who we are and where our talents lie.

Now, not every passion is something that you can make money from, but it is something that you can also do as a hobby to help keep you in good spirits as you are working in other areas. However, if you enjoy your nine-to-five life and it might not exactly be the thing "you're most passionate about", then it's okay to just have that passion as a side hobby that you do for fun.

For me, I did have to take a step back because I wasn't happy in my place of work. I was getting physically sick from the stress of not having a true work-life balance, being in a toxic work environment, and not doing something I actually loved. And I rarely get sick. I felt like I was wasting my time and just did not want to be in that job anymore. Although I liked the company overall, and most people I worked with – I was checked out, disengaged, giving 0 *efs*.

I had a Black boss who I felt didn't know she was Black because of her other identities taking precedence. She wasn't really giving the development I needed – partly because she wasn't set up for success in her role as a manager either. George

Floyd's murder had just transpired, and as you know, being Black at work was just hard. More than it normally was.

I wasn't treating my loved ones fairly and was subconsciously taking out my frustrations on them.

So also take a moment to see where you are on that scale in your current situation.

Are you feeling burnt out?

Are you checked out?

Are you disengaged?

Are you counting down the time until you can stop doing whatever it is that you're doing?

Are you treating the people you care about poorly? Check in with them to see.

These are all key indicators that maybe you should shift your focus elsewhere and use your time and talent more wisely.

For me, that looked like quitting my 6 figure, nine-to-five career and pursuing my coaching while still figuring out what was best for me. This meant I was taking more time to research and learn about the other areas that I may want to take a job in or eventually create businesses in for myself. It was a struggle at points and is still a struggle sometimes. However, I took a chance on myself and realized I could write this book and touch the lives of millions. I also realized that if I were to work in a company, it needed to be in specialized areas that played to my strengths, not the generalist roles I did before. I'm taking control of my career the way *I* want to do it. And for that, I couldn't be happier.

Now, quitting the nine-to-five life isn't for everyone. Especially when you haven't 100% planned everything out. This is why I say take a moment to reflect on how your previous experiences have impacted you, the feelings you have associated with those experiences, if you want to continue down the career path you're on, or if you want to change industries, roles, or businesses.

Are you burnt out and over it, or do you just need a moment of rest to recoup before getting back at it?

Think about what your passions are and if you're pursuing those. If you aren't, why not?

Lastly, think about what your motivation is.

Why do you want to pursue this specific career path? Why is it important to you, your family, or your community? Is the reason enough to keep you going back every day even when things get tough?

Knowing your 'why' will keep you pushing forward, being intentional, disciplined, and consistent even when you don't want to.

And if you know your 'why,' write it out and put it somewhere visible to make sure that when you're ready to throw in the towel, you can look at it and remind yourself of the bigger picture.

You should ask yourself these questions to know how to pivot from where you are now. Knowing your 'why' is crucial to figuring out what you need to do to take that next step. Then you can take a moment to see if your career compass is facing the right direction. And if so, you can begin to build out your goals which we will discuss next.

CHAPTER 3

Are you S.M.A.R.T.?

Since we were able to reflect on what motivates us, what our passions are, and how we feel about our previous experiences, we can now ask ourselves, "What is the next move we want to make?"

This is where we can start to lay out our goals. Now, we are taught to make S.M.A.R.T. goals because you're more likely to complete them and attain them than if you just have something abstract.

This is true, and we'll need to make sure that we don't allow elements of fear and restriction to affect these goals.

So let's dive in to see what I mean.

So what is a S.M.A.R.T. goal?

In a nutshell, it stands for Specific, Measurable, Attainable/Achievable, Realistic/Relevant, and Timely.

1. Specific

The start of any S.M.AR.T. goal is to make sure that it is something specific and pointed. This will help you stay focused, and you will know the end goal you desire to obtain.

For example:

If you just say, "I want to make a lot of money," that can look like anything. Also, a lot of money is relative. To someone making $2 an hour, having $15 an hour is a lot of money. However, to someone who makes $50 an hour on salary, $15 an hour isn't much.

Therefore, you need to narrow down what "a lot of money" means. Instead, you can say, "I want to make $200,000 by October of next year." That is more specific, and it leads to the other points of having a timeline and something that's measurable.

2. Measurable

For a goal to be measurable, there needs to be some indicator that you're making progress. If you want to make two hundred thousand dollars by next October, then perhaps the way you measure that is to figure out your income each month. If you decide that you want to become a manager, measuring if you're meeting specific qualifications as you progress in your current role will be helpful.

Having a measurable goal is pretty self-explanatory. But there are tools you can utilize to ensure that you are measuring them efficiently based on your goal. If you want to manage your time better, then getting a planner will be helpful as a tool for you to achieve that.

3. Attainable/Achievable

This is making sure the goal you set is something you can do. It can stretch you, but if it's too far out of reach - it won't be attainable.

Your goal may be to be a director in your function. If you have mapped out the specific path and can measure if you are on track from entry-level to manager to director, then it is something you will view as attainable. When we have confidence in attaining our goals, we are more likely to achieve them.

4. Realistic / Relevant

I put both words here because it can vary depending on where you look up what a S.M.A.R.T. goal is. So you can determine which one you'd like to abide by or which one will help you better achieve whatever your S.M.A.R.T. goal is because there is a difference between the two.

If you have a goal of $200,000 by October of next year and are implementing all of the things that will help you get there, it's considered realistic; just like you wanting to be a director and laying out the masterplan and taking action to get there will also make that realistic.

Now looking at relevancy, your goals should align with your values and passions. If you're setting a goal that truly goes against your character, then that goal won't be something that's relevant to you and what you're truly trying to accomplish in life.

For example, if I value making the world a better place, but then I take a job with a company known for polluting the environment or even supporting injustices like police brutality, then my work isn't relevant or aligned with my views or what I feel is important. Better yet, if you decide to be a director but keep taking on projects that won't get you better visibility or build the needed skills, you aren't aligned with your goal, and your choices are lacking in relevance.

The goals you set for yourself should have some type of relevance to your core values or what you envision for your career.

5. Timely

This last one deals with the time frame that it'll take for you to reach the said goal that you set for yourself. Now I am huge on deadlines because they help me hold my clients accountable for something they say they're going to do. As humans, we tend to be a bit lazy, so we need to trick our minds into being motivated to do what we desire. If I just say I want $200,000 and don't give myself a deadline, then I'll probably never reach the goal of having $200,000 because I'm just going to take all the time in the world.

If you want to be a director in your function but don't try to get promotions within a specific amount of time, take on projects, or connect with the right people, you'll most likely be stuck and never reach that goal.

S.M.A.R.T. goals are helpful to point you in the right direction when setting goals for yourself. As you write out each letter, I caution you not to throw in unnecessary doubts or fears. Use the acronym as a guideline to help you navigate your career, but if you decide to do something that may seem unattainable or unrealistic, just take a step back and assess if it's because it's coming from a place of fear or because it truly has nothing to do with your overarching aim in life or within your career.

However, before we can dictate whether or not your goals are considered S.M.A.R.T., we have to set some initial goals. Think about where you are in your career right now.

- Do you want to be promoted to a new position within your current company?
- If so, what positions are you looking for?
- What does a promotion look like for your work-life balance?
- Are you ready to take on the type of work that comes with it?

Do you want to change careers?
- If so, have you thought about the different industries and why?
- Do you know people in the new industry or career path that you're trying to pursue?
- Do you have any experience in this new area?

These are just a few questions to get your mind going.

As you ponder these things, sit down and start to write out some goals you have for yourself in each of these areas. Then use the S.M.A.R.T. method to gauge how close you are to meeting them, but don't necessarily hold back even if they seem "outside of the box" or "unrealistic" to other people (and even to yourself initially). Go big or go home is my motto!

Development Plans

Another thing to think about if you are working a nine-to-five is to look at what you identified in your IDP at work (Individual Development Plan).

Normally, within your IDP, you outline your goals for the next 3 to 5 years at the said job so that your manager can help guide you to take the specific roles or build the capabilities needed to reach whatever goals you have. Make sure you are working with your manager to achieve what you set out and get the development that will help you along the way. If you aren't being developed, that's a completely different conversation. Don't be afraid to involve outside stakeholders who will help get you where you need to be and who want to see you thrive.

If your goal is eventually to be the vice president of snacks within your company, then it would be wise to work as a marketing/brand manager on a brand within snacks at some point.

You probably could also learn about consumer insights by having one of those roles to get a broader picture and understanding of what happens within that space.

If you're in HR (human resources), which I was as a business partner, you support different functions. So you can be a generalist or a specialist within HR. We could say if you wanted to be a director-level at some point, then maybe you should support finance, take another role supporting marketing, and then build from there.

If you're within the supply chain, you may need to make sure you support operations at some point and then support engineering to get a full grasp of what's needed within that space. You can also be a business partner to logistics just so you can better help those functions. When you're a director, you can better tell your managers how to handle their people within those different spaces because you understand what it means to be in those positions.

Mentors & Coaches

It is very helpful to have a mentor or coach within the space that you are working in. Having someone who has been where you're at and is successful and willing to share their knowledge with you and help guide you along your journey is vital and will be pivotal to your career.

It is said that it takes a village, which is true if you want to advance. No one gets to where they want to be on their own.

Mentors are people (or even concepts from books) who help guide you in your development. They can be sounding boards. They can show you how to accomplish a goal. They can walk you through the steps they took for success. They can help you brainstorm life goals and connect you with other people who can help.

Some mentors will come free (money-wise), and others will come with a price. Either way, their relationship is invaluable. I didn't have to pay my initial mentors. I was fortunate enough to find them through different avenues and asked them to be a mentor. Again, they were people in similar spaces I wanted to be in. As of recently, some of my mentors have been paid because they have larger mentorship programs.

Coaches, on the other hand, are accountability partners who guide you along your journey to help you meet your goals. They help you push past your limiting beliefs, challenge you to set deadlines for your goals, cheer you on, and celebrate you along the way. They provide you with the tools to succeed and should be certified in their craft and/or have relevant experience in the field. There are a lot of people claiming to be coaches when in fact they are more like mentors or advisors. Do your research to know the difference. The International Coaching Federation breaks down what a true coach is and lists the accredited coaching programs people go through since they are the "gold standard" for coaching.

I also join mastermind groups and go through different programs that will help me within my businesses. They are with people that I watched in interviews and now am rubbing elbows with (literally). They are folks who are bringing in multimillions within their businesses and can help me to do the same. They are folks who create a community and allow you to grow together. Remember: there is power in proximity.

Connect with people of all levels and don't feel like they won't bring you value. It could be something as simple as their experience as a Black employee at the company that can help you shift your goal in a different direction. They can discuss the nuances of the roles and help you narrow down your career trajectory for when you speak to someone in a higher position. Always be willing to learn and share with others as you grow.

Remember that sometimes the advice you receive should be taken with a grain of salt; sometimes, some of those people might not understand your overall goals and may try to deter you, depending on the situation. So that's why you need to make sure that if you have mentors and coaches, they align to a specific area and understand your goals and your purpose so that they can help. At the end of the day, the things you are doing are for you, your reasons, your family, and your freedom. Just check to make sure that the advice rings true to your values or that your decisions align with who you are.

A quick example of this will be when one of my mentors introduced me to one of his friends with the caveat that this person was a little eccentric and may or may not align with what I had going on - so to basically take the meeting with them with a grain of salt.

We ended up having a phone call, and I told them what I was trying to do with my coaching. This person wasn't 100% on the same page. They were speaking to things that weren't necessarily in the lane that I was trying to get into and told me how I needed more street credit. To a degree, they were right, but not necessarily in the sense they were speaking to it. They seemed to be discouraging because they were comparing me to a huge corporation where their spouse worked in a somewhat similar space but at a higher and broader level.

They were trying to compare me to a huge conglomerate that wasn't necessarily targeting the same area or niche. Therefore, I took that bit of it with a grain of salt. However, the conversation did a few things for me. One - it lit a fire under me to truly realize why I am more than qualified for my work and the value I bring. Two - it helped me realize that not everyone will get it, and that's okay. I can still have them in my network but maybe develop that relationship differently. Lastly - I should think of my company in terms of where I want it to be and not necessarily where it is now.

You can always take a lesson out of any conversation, even if it's one that doesn't necessarily help you at the moment but can bring something beneficial for the long haul.

So for you in your job, think of where you want your overall career to go, not just what's happening now. Move with the end goal in mind and know that these are the S.M.A.R.T. steps you take to get there.

CHAPTER 4

Let's Talk about Strengths Baby!

Many of us go through life not thinking about our accomplishments or strengths until perhaps we're sitting in an interview. When you take a moment to sit and reflect on your strengths, that's just one more way to build up that positive muscle in your mind.

It'll also help you when you're starting to have these conversations with people who may be outside your network and don't know much about you. Speaking on your strengths can come in handy if you have a specific skill-set that others might not have in that area. And even if they have that skill, only you can bring it to the table how YOU do it. That's your value add.

I want to emphasize this chapter, especially as Black professionals, because we tend to downplay ourselves and undervalue ourselves, especially in the corporate setting. We tend to shrink back and allow others to get the glory for the hard work we've done. We tend not to "sell ourselves" as well as our other counterparts. We tend to allow companies to mistreat us and drain all of our energy with nothing but mental and physical health issues to show for it.

So walking through the steps and understanding the importance of knowing your strengths is super important to move forward the way you want in your career.

When I was helping another one of my clients in Ghana who wanted to re-enter the workforce, part of our sessions was to figure out what value she brought to the table and her different strengths.

I often like to ask certain questions, which I will list out later in the chapter, to have people think outside of the box around things that they may not realize are something valuable and unique to them. Through this process, as we were talking, she listed a few things and then said that she realized she was great at being resourceful to get the job done, especially around building & utilizing her relationships across multiple functions. That is strength, especially if it's something that other people don't naturally do. So we are talking about things that can help set you apart from other folks who may be in similar positions or who may have similar skill sets.

There's always something unique to you that only you can do the way you do it. Only YOU have experienced your life. So no one can take that away from you because they aren't you. They don't know what you know in the manner that you know it. These are the things we will touch on within this chapter and beyond.

I want you to think about how often you currently write down your accomplishments or even your strengths. These can be either personal or professional.

If you find yourself saying that you don't really write these things down, that's okay because most people don't do it either.

I previously didn't do it until it came time to apply for a new role! But this is where we will help you differentiate yourself from others.

As you get new projects, roles, etc., write down the capabilities you have for these things. Write down what you've achieved within these spaces and what you've helped others and your company to achieve.

Take it a step further and go through your life from a younger age and write down the milestones or pivots or situations where your strengths came through or influenced something or had some accomplishment. This is an exercise my business coach had me do, and it helped me to think about things that I had completely forgotten about but were situations where I helped a group of people or made some type of difference.

I'll even challenge you to write down some of the "failures" you've had along the way. Projects that didn't go well, times where you struggled or it was challenging to fulfill your goal. These types of questions will also come up in your interviews. It's good to know the moments you took a risk, failed, or had some type of conflict in completing a project or task. After you think of those, write what you learned from those experiences. That is the money. That is what people will look for. It's not about the failure itself; it's about what you did after the fact and how you applied what you learned to the next project or role.

Make a habit of writing these accomplishments and experiences down monthly, quarterly, or even more than that. It could be bi-weekly, depending on what you're doing. But you need to write down any accomplishments and areas of opportunity for that self awareness, especially as you are getting new projects or having some type of shift within your work. This way, when it does come time to apply to a new role, or you go to a networking event and talk to somebody, you have these things top of mind, and it's easier to speak about versus having to rack your brain to think of the plethora of things you've done over the last two years.

What I want you to do now is pause, sit down, and take the time to write your accomplishments from the last few years and the strengths that helped you achieve these things.

You can separate it by the different roles you've held if that makes it easier or the different companies you worked for.

You could also take a strengthsfinder test online to help you hone in on some strengths that you weren't sure about. Just make sure that it's well-vetted because some of these tests or assessments can be generic based on your answers. If you had to do something like this in school or for your job, which can also include a personality test, feel free to utilize those when you're thinking about your different strengths for this next portion.

Next, I want you to answer these 4 questions. Write down 3 answers for each.

1. What things do you get complimented on? What strengths can underlie?
2. What do you do better than others?
3. What challenges have you overcome? What strengths could be associated?

4. When have you been criticized for something that was actually a strength (e.g., if you were told to stay out of grown folks' business as a child, it could be that you have an inquisitive nature which is great for research, gaining insights, analyzing data, etc.)?

Other areas you can think about are the feedback you received from someone else. Like when you have your performance review with your manager or one-on-one meetings. What are some things they say that can be attributed to your strengths? What are you doing well? What have you improved upon?

Ask your family members or friends about some strengths they believe you have or things that they are always congratulating you on.

CHAPTER 5

What's Your Value?

The next step is utilizing everything from the previous chapter and putting it together into a brand statement. But before we get to that, let's break down exactly what a brand is.

Most times, when we think of a brand, we normally picture a company or clothing line or something of that nature. If I asked you right now what your favorite brand is, you might say something like Nike, Ben & Jerry's, Fashion Nova, or Black by Popular Demand.

So then, what is a brand? For a company, it's the value they bring to their customer and a bit of their personality.

For example: Cheerios (which itself is a brand of General Mills).

- What do you normally think about when it comes to cheerios?
- Is it positive or negative?
- How are they servicing their customers? Is it valuable?

Let's break it down:

- When I think of Cheerios - initially, it's as "baby's first food." Whenever you think of a baby/toddler transitioning into their first solid foods, they have a box of cheerios dumped out in front of them with their parents watching gleefully as they stuff a handful into their face.
- This is a positive thought and a happy one.
- The value is that, as a parent, I can trust Cheerios as a safe brand of food for my baby to eat.
- I also must feel that the cereal is healthy enough to introduce to my baby.
- Another piece of their brand is that they are heart-healthy and help lower cholesterol. We've all seen the commercials with Buzz Bee. So overall, Cheerios is a safe, healthy, and family-friendly brand from the time you are a toddler to when you are a senior citizen.

Now let's utilize the same strategy as we think about brands for people: AKA personal brands. Your personal brand is the essence of who you are. It's what you stand for. It's what you bring to the table. It's your value.

The best part is that you can use your personal brand to influence your career!

Your brand will come through in everything you're doing, whether it's networking, interviewing, your resume, LinkedIn, etc.; your brand will be reflected in all of those things, and it should be succinct and tell the same story.

You want to make sure that you control the narrative of your story because it is your life; it's your strengths, your capabilities, and the value that you're bringing to the table. There is often a perception versus reality when it comes to somebody's brand, *ESPECIALLY* as a Black professional. You know by now that we tend to be labeled as the "angry black..." "uncooperative..." "not a team player..." "aggressive..." you get the idea.

So we need to protect our brand and reputation because others will be quick to paint the narrative for you (especially in a negative light) if you let them.

For example, when it's time for performance reviews, managers within the department often come together and evaluate all of their employees against one another - which means you're being evaluated against your peers. So when the question comes up of "how is so and so doing?" it can either go one of two ways: your manager can reply, "Oh, they're super hard working; they're really great at building relationships with other people in the department; they're such a team player"... blasé, blasé. Or they could say something along the lines of "They're really difficult to work with; they don't really put forth an effort; I haven't seen much progress since they've started"... blah blah blah.

I had a positive example of this happen to me when I was interning at a Fortune 500 company during my MBA. We were probably four or so weeks in as I was continuing to build out my network within the company. And this company is huge on relationships; for me, being a relationship cultivator and connector is part of my brand. So I reached out to the Chief Human Resources Officer and asked her for a coffee chat so we could connect. I had done this at the advice of a mentor who used to work at the company as the VP of Snacks. So I didn't really realize at the moment that she was in the c-suite because they had two titles next to her name within our system. I didn't think twice about it until my manager came up to me a day or so later and asked if I had reached out to her.

He told me that I was not in trouble, but just to make sure in the future, to run something like that by him first because his manager came to him and informed him that the CHRO was asking about me. So fast forward, I ended up meeting with her, and she told me that she decided to meet with me because she asked around about me (aka, my brand preceded me). She didn't know who I was and was wondering if it was worth her time, which obviously you can imagine she's a very busy woman. So when she reached out to my boss's manager's boss and other directors and VPS within HR who I had already built relationships with, they gave her great feedback about me and the work that I was doing and that she should meet with me. So as we sat there, we discussed personal life, work-life stuff, and the different projects I was working on. She seemed very excited about it and was impressed with what I was doing as it would directly affect a new structure that the company was putting in place within their plants.

Clearly, my personal brand was working in my favor because it got me a seat at the table with the Chief Human Resources Officer, whom my manager never even spoke to and his manager never even had a meeting with! And they had been at the company for years! The fact that I had built these relationships with the people *she* trusted and knew is what got my foot in the door. My strength in building relationships (which we'll discuss later) and the fact that the company values relationships helped me influence my internship. Also, the fact that I was working on the talent team and the work I did involved developing new leaders was also a bonus (another piece of my brand, which is talent development).

This is the type of stuff that I'm talking about when I say that you need to bet on yourself, not have a spirit of fear, and take certain risks. No other intern had a personal one-on-one with her, and they all thought I was crazy when I told them what had happened. This was "outside of the box." From the way they told it, I had gone over everybody's head to get a meeting with this woman.

Now, if I had followed protocol when it comes to speaking to someone within that high of a position, I probably would have never met with this woman because I'm sure my manager would say, "no, she's too busy," or "just wait until you guys have an intern meeting and she shows up" or any other excuse to discourage me, because to them, me meeting with the CHRO would have been an unrealistic and unattainable goal. Do you see how it's all starting to connect?

I ensured that my brand, which was being a relationship builder and a talent developer, was coming through in everything I was doing. Also, when they were having those behind-the-scenes conversations about me, no one could say anything bad. It resulted in me meeting with one of the people with the highest positions in our company and influence within my function. And with that being said, and her actually liking me, that meant I probably was guaranteed to get an offer from that internship because now I have the CHRO on my side unless - I completely did something to ef up during the summer (and I did get the full-time offer and the location of my choice FYI).

That is how I influenced my career being an intern who had only been at the company for three to four weeks. That is how I set myself in a position where I could meet with the CHRO and develop relationships with different directors and VPS for me to be able to have that meeting, and to secure my internship offer for full time. And you better believe that nobody else in the whole intern class (in any function) did anything like that. I was even chosen to represent the intern class at World Headquarters for a podcast the company was doing on the company's influence on interns' career trajectories.

So - now that we're starting to make everything connect, let's go back to what you wrote down from the previous chapter around your strengths and the answers to those questions. Based on this information, we will put together your brand statement:

What common themes did you keep coming to within those answers?

Do you find yourself running from these areas, or are you leaning into them?

I ask this question because sometimes we run away from our strengths and things we are passionate about. Sometimes we feel that those things don't hold a current place in what we're trying to do. If you are great at public speaking but are always avoiding the opportunity to speak up and present, you are running from your strength. You might be well known for being an orator, but if you never volunteer to give the keynote or present for a project, you are missing out on various opportunities that could come from you doing so.

If I were to describe my value in a nutshell, it is that I am a talent developer who naturally builds strong relationships and connections while advocating for the liberation of minds. If I want to go deeper with it, my brand within my company is that I empower black millennials (and working professionals) to propel their careers and increase their earning potential through building their confidence in their professional and networking skills.

I am empowering people to build professional skills in the talent development portion of my brand and the relationship building portion because I have to foster a relationship with my clients. I also help them foster new relationships with people as they network to reach their goals. The liberation aspect comes through in the fact that I'm helping them take control of a career that they love; therefore, they are being liberated to navigate an environment of their choosing and that they are passionate about - not one that was told to them. I am also helping people liberate their minds from the constraints that society has put on us and the traumas we have experienced that could be holding us down.

So put together a statement that encompasses and embodies your value and skill sets based on what you've gathered. Use those strengths. Use those questions that I asked. Pinpoint the top values you are bringing to the table (or want to bring to the table). There can also be action verbs within your statement, just like I have "I empower... to build." It honestly should be action-oriented because it describes your essence and what you offer to the world.

Once you have your statement, look at it and ask yourself if it captures your value? If not, refine it. Your personal brand statement is living, and you can continue to iterate it as you strengthen your capabilities and grow in your values. But the core of it and of who you are will somewhat be the same, just like any version of my brand statements will encompass development, relationship building, and some form of liberation of your mental state and confidence.

You can then reflect and decide if you can speak to your value with confidence, and speak to the statement with confidence... and speak to your strengths with confidence. Can you talk about your achievements with confidence?

You should be able to do this if you want to work with other people or gain employment because folks always want to know what value you can add. And you should know what you value about yourself and the things that you've done. You should be proud of that, speak to it, and let people know that you are more than capable and that they do need your service.

This is probably the biggest area of improvement I've seen amongst Black working professionals (and even entrepreneurs). We tend to sell ourselves short and undervalue ourselves. I had a manager (white woman) tell me that she wasn't really trying to promote one of her employees because she never spoke up for herself (Black woman). Meanwhile, the Black employee was telling everyone else she felt undervalued but wouldn't even talk to the manager about it for them to address it head-on. She also came off as someone who lacked confidence and would let other people overtalk her. The crazy thing is, she was doing great work!

Maybe it comes from the centuries of being berated and being told that we wouldn't amount to anything, so those feelings have passed down through the generations. It also definitely comes back to what we spoke about in chapter one around refining our minds and not operating in trauma, fear, or projections others have imposed on us.

I was a keynote speaker for multiple women's organizations, and during one of the workshops where we focused on building our brands, a young woman mentioned how hard it was for her to speak to her value. She was raised in a household where it was seen as rude to talk about herself positively that way. People saw it as being conceited. So she initially struggled to write her brand statement, but when she did, it was amazing! It was a mental barrier that she had to override. The women in the session had to refine their minds in order to complete the exercise.

We tend to shy away from our true values. And in the situation at my job, I definitely had to coach both the manager and the employee to communicate with one another and ensure folks are valued for their work.

Let this book be a reminder that you are worth it. You are more than enough. You are more than capable. Let this book be a reminder that your talents are great and someone out there needs them. You are Black and beautiful. You are wonderfully made.

There is nothing arrogant or cocky about it. Many of us have grown up in environments where it's frowned upon to speak about ourselves because it might come off as bragging, like the young lady from my workshop. But if you want to get ahead, you need to know how to speak about yourself; it's not bragging if you're not trying to put others down and make them feel bad. It's you speaking to your own self-worth and value and being excited to share that with the world.

You can also look to see what skills and capabilities you need to brush up on. Do you need to take some courses, get certifications, or anything else to help you build up your skills and value?

Do you need a coach like myself to help you build out whatever those skill sets are? Again, I help Black (and working) professionals build confidence in their professional (knowing and speaking to your value, personal branding, interviewing, etc.) and networking (relationship building, utilization of those relationships, etc.) skills. You can gain access to my online coaching program and masterclasses at www.therecruitrefinery.com/services.

This is a good reminder from the last chapter to set dates for yourself of when you're going to keep track of your accomplishments within your job to reflect back on.

It's also a good time to remember to set a date or specific times during the month where you affirm yourself. The two work in tandem because the more you can affirm yourself, the more positive your mindset, and the easier it will be to speak to your worth and value. I tend to say my affirmations each morning as a constant reminder of who I am and to give myself positive vibes as I meditate. Make sure you practice speaking to your skills and capabilities to feel natural when you're talking to people. Also, so that you can remember how great you are and all the wonderful things you have done up until this point, that you're capable of doing now, and will be capable of doing in the future.

CHAPTER 6

Tell Me about Yourself

By this point, you should be feeling pretty great about yourself. You should be excited to share with others all of your great experiences and the things you've done and the value you bring to the table. Now we will shift into crafting your story so you can do just that.

The question that we will be answering is something that you hear all the time, regardless of whether you're meeting somebody new for the first time at a party or sitting in front of somebody at an interview. Everyone wants to know and will ask you to tell them about yourself.

This is where many people drop the ball because, somehow, this question throws them off. As I mentioned earlier, we aren't conditioned to speak about ourselves, so we tend to feel icky and weird when asked to do so. Because of that, people don't take the time to think about who they are and what makes them valuable and powerful while being able to explain that to a stranger. But we want that stranger to hire us for a role or a job? If you struggle to relay the most basic information about yourself in order to help people understand who you are, how will we find the areas where we can align? How can I relate to you so that I want to foster a deeper relationship?

So again, I'm going to ask, "Tell me about yourself?"

What is your first impulse reaction? Are you cringing right now? Are you feeling nervous? Or do you have some idea of what you would say when presented with this question?

This question can cost a lot of people an opportunity to get a role because when you start fumbling around and you're not very confident when asked about yourself, how can one be confident that you can do what they need you to do?

Today, we are going to break that cycle, and you will craft one hell of a story about who you are in a way that makes you feel confident and allows whoever you're speaking with to know what you value and what you also bring to the table.

Essentially, your answer should be NO MORE than 3 minutes long (with 1-2 minutes as the sweet spot), and you could cut it up into a 30-second elevator pitch if need be. That's how detailed and well thought out it is and how concise it should be.

When someone is asking you to tell them about yourself, the best thing to consider is that there are three things you should touch on: where you've been, where you are currently, and where you're going.

This sounds easy enough, right? Wrong. Because if it were this easy half of the people who answer it during an interview or otherwise wouldn't fail so miserably. It's such a simple question but can bring about much complexity. This is because many people don't know where to begin or even where to end when asked this question. It's so open-ended that you might not give enough information about what you have going on, or you might give too much information. You might speak about something that's completely irrelevant to the matter at hand.

When I hosted an interviewing masterclass focused on this question, one of the students on the call fell into this trap. On her first go-around, she probably gave me three to four sentences of who she was, and I still didn't have a clear sense of what was going on. There was the normal "this is where I'm from" piece of the answer, and then a quick "this is what I do now" and maybe half of a phrase about what is wanted from the future.

The most important reason why most people tend to fail at this question is that they truly don't know who they are. That is why I emphasized getting your mind right, setting out your values, and building that brand statement. Because you've done this, it'll be easier to share with someone who you are because you've done the work ahead of time to know for yourself.

This is your opportunity to truly engage whoever you're speaking to because many times, people are also looking to see if you have anything in common or if they can relate to anything that you're speaking on. Now, it's not your job to try to fish out what the commonalities are within your stories when you're speaking about yourself initially. Eventually, as you ask them the same question and they go through their story, you'll see from your end that you'll be looking for things that you have in common as well. It's because that is what will make you trust them more and feel better about talking to them and working with them.

Let's dive in and break this question down so that you can have much success the next time somebody asks you, "Tell me about yourself?"

1. Where have you been?

In this section, you're going to give a brief synopsis of how you started your journey. You can state where you're from; you can talk about what college you went to, what you studied there, how that impacted you, and any clubs or jobs you held during that time of importance. You will also discuss any pivots that were important to and in alignment with your personal brand.

Something like this for me would go:

"I'm originally from Indianapolis, Indiana. After high school, I moved down to Atlanta to attend Spelman College, the number one HBCU (Historically Black College & University) in the nation, where I majored in Spanish pre-med. I wanted to become a pediatric cardiovascular surgeon who worked within Black and Latino communities and with Doctors Without Borders.

In my junior year, I studied abroad in Argentina and was exposed to so many new things as it was my first time living out of the country. At that time, I started wavering whether I truly wanted to attend medical school. So as graduation time came around, I decided to take a gap year and move to Chicago, where I taught algebra 1 and algebra 2 to high school freshmen and sophomores and helped them gain confidence in their intelligence as well as in their identities as Black youth. I realized through that experience that I didn't need to go into medicine to have a direct impact on people's lives, and I was beginning to realize my love of developing others."

So that is just an example of a snippet of what I would say for the 'where I've been piece;' I'd give or take some information, then start to transition into where I am now.

So you want to think of the "where you've been" portion of the 'tell me about yourself' as the setting or set up to the climax for your story. Think of this as your origin story for all of the comic book and manga nerds out there. This is the piece that helped develop you into who you are today: just like Batman experienced trauma by seeing his parents murdered by a robber as a child. It led him to be a vigilante to keep the streets safe, and in the future, assuming he would want to inspire other people to also keep the city safe and whatnot... this isn't an exact science to the DC Universe, but you get what I mean; stuff like that.

From this piece of my story alone, I've been able to intrigue every interviewer I have ever spoken to and had a percentage of the interview focused on my travels abroad and the fact that I wanted to go into medicine (somehow, most of my interviewers also dabbled in the medical field and changed course). Therefore, they found me relatable and were excited to learn more about this piece of my life and to relay a bit of their own experiences. I also have a more "nontraditional" background, which is intriguing for folks.

2. Where are you now?

This piece of the story is what you're currently doing. So after you give that nice little background about yourself, now we're going to talk about the current job that you're in or the type of projects you work on. You can go into any groups that you're a part of or organizations that you volunteer with, any boards that you're sitting on, and how that plays into what you just said about yourself.

If there was some pivotal point that caused you to change your trajectory or that's happening currently that will make you change your trajectory, this is where you tee that up.

So, for example, the next portion of my story would go something like this:

"I recently left my job as an HR business partner at a Fortune 500 company and am now full-time in my career coaching. I'm empowering black millennials to propel their careers by building confidence in their professional and networking skills, as working professionals. I work with folks who want to re-enter the workforce, promote their jobs, or change careers, although one of my first clients ended up pivoting into starting a new business after we began working together.

I am continuing to hone my craft through staying up to date on job market information through my contracted coaching positions and HR network and platforms to give my clients real-time advice."

You can see that I'm speaking about the things that have happened currently within the past year to now; that is what I would say is pretty current, or you can maybe even go like two years back; that's still pretty "current;" you can talk about how the pandemic affected you or your role at work.

If you're somebody who lost your job, then you can discuss the things you've learned during this time, any hobbies or skills you've built up since then, and so on and so forth. The intention here would be to focus on asset-based conversations rather than deficits. You always want to ensure you can turn a negative situation into a learning or positive outcome.

3. Where you're going

Lastly, you're going to discuss where you plan to go: where everything to this point is leading you next based on what you've learned through your experiences and what you value.

Now you can start to discuss any other pivots that you plan to make or how this role will help you do xyz. You can discuss what you plan to bring to the company or the department you're talking to, depending on if you're interviewing or just networking - whatever is right for that situation.

My example would be something to this effect:

"Now that I've worked with some clients and I understand that the business I have is a need, I want to touch more people that may not necessarily be connected to me through social media or my network. I am writing a book where I walk people through the necessary steps that will help them gain career success even without my direct coaching. I want to put the information out there that I've learned through my experience as an

HR professional sitting at the table with managers, influencing their hiring decisions, and knowing the behind the scenes of why they would or wouldn't hire/promote someone.

I am looking to bring my talents to a more structured environment, working within a company to help their pool of Black employees in early career to mid-management positions so that they can build that pipeline that they desire. Currently, companies are having issues with developing their Black talent. That's where I would come in and teach them those professional skills and help them to get mentors and champions, learn how to speak to their values, and know what they've done in their current positions to push them to that next step of getting that promotion and moving up the ladder."

Here, I'm speaking about what I want and the value I will bring to whoever I plan to connect with in the future. It doesn't matter whether or not these things actually happen. This is your goal and your plans, right? Folks want to see that you are forward-thinking. You always want to make sure that you are connecting your value to whoever or whatever it is that you're speaking to because if you only just talk about what you hope to gain, then you're going to leave them thinking, "Okay, but what do we get?" "Why should we listen? Why should we partner?" You really want to answer, "So what?" when giving the last portion of your answer—the result of everything that's led up to this point.

To circle back to my student from earlier, I had her re-tell me about herself after I explained these concepts to her and we broke them down. This time, she gave a much more detailed answer after thinking on it for a few minutes, and it allowed me to see much more of her passions and capabilities. Even though she still needed to give more details on the "where are you going?" portion, it was a much clearer picture, and I found myself connecting to different parts of her story. She also felt much more confident in her new statement and could see the difference in the impact.

Make sure you go back over this chapter multiple times and the last couple of chapters. You want to make sure you are truly crafting your story to engage your listener, and to help them see the things that you value and are passionate about, on top of how you can be of service to one another. If you notice, my brand is woven throughout that story as someone who values developing talent and building relationships. Sometimes these conversations aren't necessarily to get a job. It might be to connect with someone else who can help you achieve what you're trying to do. This goes back to the example of when I was speaking with my mentor about what I wanted to do in my business, and he connected me with somebody who was in a similar space regardless of whether it worked or not. These are the types of things that you want to think about as you're moving through your career as a working professional. Your network is your net worth, and that is what I will be speaking about next.

CHAPTER 7

What is Networking *Really?*

Networking has long been dreaded by people for dozens of years. We're used to thinking of drab, boring meetings in a hotel conference room where everyone's dressed up in suits and ties and uncomfortable black pumps as they speak awkwardly with one another about their goals and the uncertain future ahead.

However, I am here to tell you that there is way more to networking than just that scene we replay repeatedly in our minds as soon as someone says the word. Networking can be fun, and it comes in different forms, not just in a hotel conference room.

So if you're one of these people who cringe every time they hear the word networking, keep reading, and let's see if we can change your mind about the concept as a whole.

Networking is vital regardless of what field you find yourself in. Even as a child, you were networking with your classmates on the first day of school, during summer camp, or when you were joining a sports team. You have to network to get to know people in order to work together.

Unless you go through life like the bubble boy trapped in a space all by yourself, or you end up like Will Smith in "I am

Legend" in a city all alone, you will have to interact with other people. Therefore, you're going to have to network to some capacity.

The purpose of networking is to meet new people who can help you accomplish your goals, exchange knowledge, build a friendship, get a mentor or a mentee, and add value to one another's lives.

There are two types of networking in my book: in-person or virtual, and they each have two different categories that can fall underneath them: professional or informal.

1. In-person and professional

This first type is the one that we all know very well. It's the one where we imagine everybody in a boring, uptight manner, dressed in a suit in a conference room, feeling awkward and wanting to run in the other direction. It's the reason we all dread hearing the word networking in the first place. And this may have been made worse just by watching movies, hearing other people's horror experiences, or even reflecting on your own. However, just like the rest, it doesn't have to be dreadful, and it doesn't have to be scary.

Some examples are as follows:

- A conference for your workplace
- A conference for an organization that you volunteer for or are involved with in some way
- Fundraisers for a specific cause
- Career fairs or business school conferences

There are others for sure, but we get the gist with this list. In all of these situations, you are either trying to find a job, meet with other people in your company to gain more exposure, network with different people to figure out if their organization or school is a fit for you and if you are a fit for them, and so on.

Now when I speak to most people, they are terrified of networking and will normally find themselves in the corner of a room just watching everyone else and not speaking to anyone, especially if they are at the event alone. Other people may find themselves only sticking around the people they know and not interacting at all with the hundreds of folks in the room with them from other offices, companies, other schools, what have you. Everybody is nervous to some degree, so if you think about it that way, there is no reason for you to be nervous because, more often than not, the person you're talking to is also nervous.

Where are these nerves coming from, and why do we feel this way? A lot of times, it's because you don't know what to say, how to make small talk, or you're so pressed to make a great impression that you end up forgetting everything that you practice and make a fool of yourself. If you're clumsy, you might be struggling to eat, drink, and speak all at the same time. Therefore, you stand away and finish eating and drinking before you talk to people, or you talk to people before you start to eat and drink and the moment someone interrupts you while you're doing one or the other, you feel completely lost and like you've been backed into a corner.

So we'll come back to how we can mitigate these after I list out all of them because the solution pretty much is the same for each level; we just might have to tweak it for each situation.

Pro tip:

Find the person standing alone or sitting to themselves and approach them first. Chances are they, too, are super nervous about going to speak to other people. You can both break the ice by talking to someone else who is on the same page; then you feel more confident to start breaking into other groups of people after the fact, or you all can tackle the rest of the event together.

2. In-person and informal

This is one that people don't consider as networking because you're in such a relaxed environment that you don't put the same pressure on yourself to speak to people in the room. Sometimes folks do, especially if they're in a situation where they came alone, or they may not know as many people in attendance. But the same feeling can still creep up of feeling awkward and nervous and having a fear of making a fool of yourself. Some situations are as follows:

- Happy hour
- Birthday party
- A family gathering that isn't your own or it could be your own as well
- Going out with friends to a bar or a club

There are others, but this pretty much encompasses what we're going for.

These are normal situations where you are amongst a group of peers, or you're after work and hanging out with some coworkers and colleagues (not necessarily a company-led event).

Happy hours can be either with friends or for a work event. This one can fall into the category of being both informal and professional because anytime it's dealing with your job, there's still some type of professionalism that you want to hold.

However, this is an opportunity for you to show your personality and get to know folks on a completely different level than just having conversations around projects you're working on. Companies have learned by now that if you put alcohol in front of folks and give them free food, they are more likely to loosen up and get chatty. This, however, can suck for the minority of people in the room who don't partake in alcohol. This definitely became a thing for a semester at my business school, and we had dry happy hours because some students felt pressured to drink at the social functions. Of course, this didn't last very long because alcohol is part of the culture, and no one is forcing people to drink. They just most likely felt out of place because so many folks were doing it, or different people asked them throughout the night if they wanted a drink. I no longer partake in alcohol, although I definitely did during b-school, so I can see how folks would take it this way. However, no one cares that much, nor is holding a gun to anyone's head to have a drink.

Many conversations and business deals take place over a drink or a meal, so this is the perfect opportunity to practice these things in a somewhat safe environment. They also give you access to people you might not normally be able to reach out to daily.

If you are in real estate (realtor, investor, etc.), there are always meetups where you can come in contact with heavy hitters that may either buy or sell your properties; they could be contractors, they could be the folks that can take you to the next level. So in these situations, you are trying to network and gain information, add some value, and get some value while being somewhat professional because you're discussing business things. Still, at the same time, it's informal because everyone is relaxed and chilling. A lot of times, there are meetups at homes that are currently being fixed to be flipped or built out to be sold to a regular homeowner.

People don't think about the next events I'm about to lay out as being an opportunity to network because we always associate networking with work or business. But if you're going out to a bar with your friends, you have zero idea who you may meet that night or day. You could sit next to somebody who runs a multi-million dollar corporation, or they're in the field you're in or connected to some people you're trying to get in connection with; you just have no idea. So when you're going out, having drinks, and just enjoying yourself and making conversation with people, that is networking. The further you get into the conversation, at some point, you are going to talk about what you do for a living, or they may just start talking about different organizations that they're involved in. You may find that you have some synergy, and it's not even a work event. But you still find yourself connecting on that level that can help you excel in your career or help somebody else, and it's a great feeling. You only found it out because you were relaxed enough to speak to somebody else who you didn't know.

When it comes to family reunions and birthday parties and gatherings of that nature, there's always going to be somebody there that you: 1) have no idea how you're related, 2) don't know who they belong to, 3) never seen them before in life/didn't even know they existed. Or, you have the folks that come up and say, "I haven't seen you since you were a little child" and blah blah blah, and you have no idea who they are. So, you try to look around and figure out where your mom is or your cousin who can tell you who the hell you're talking to. But again, even in those situations, people like to stick to who they know instead of branching out to meet new family members and getting to know them and seeing what they're all about. If you're meeting your significant other's family for the first time, you have that same dreadful feeling of being nervous and not wanting to make a fool of yourself. You want them to approve of you, and you want to have a great first impression. And this is something that we'll get more into in this chapter and the next couple as well.

3. Virtual and professional

With COVID coming through and disrupting everyone's lives, everything essentially went virtual for a while, even things that folks never thought could be done in a virtual capacity. So, of course, everyone was under stay-at-home orders unless you were an essential worker (which thank you for your service if you were, especially first responders/medical workers). In my role, I was considered essential because the people that I oversaw were essential, and therefore we still had to go into the office daily, and it was not easy.

So at this point, everybody is used to this category of having department calls or one-on-one meetings with their managers or the endless Zoom calls for whatever work matters. Life didn't stop just because we had to stay at home, so people had to adapt and pivot in their current strategies and figure out how to make things work by working from home in front of a laptop if they weren't used to it.

In some of these situations, you may be on a call with a multitude of people that you may or may not know, like Town Hall meetings or even department meetings. You might not know everybody in your department and you may barely know who's on your team, depending on how large it is. You might end up having to reach out to one of those people, or you might just make note of who these people are for future reference and will end up networking with them later.

4. Virtual and informal

Because we made everything virtual, the same things that we would do in person were now done from a computer screen, such as happy hours. Many companies started doing virtual happy hours for you to still have that connection with the people in your office or even across multiple offices, allowing you to spread in that capacity. In some meetings, the organizers would do ice breakers and have people say what their drink was and a fun fact about themselves before getting into whatever the topic for the happy hour was.

Other instances are more for organizations that you may be a part of, like your local Urban League chapter, Clubhouse, or a Meetup group; these things were taking place virtually as well. So you're still in a room full of people you may or may not know, getting to know one another and coming together over a common good or topic for that evening or session. It's informal but can still play into the professional part just a bit, depending on the subject matter. These groups also hosted virtual game nights or fun activities to help people still feel like they were engaging and connecting even though they couldn't see each other in person. These are all still considered networking.

In situations where everything is new, a lot of that pressure comes from the fact that we want to make a great first impression. What are some ways that we can do that, you may ask?

Well, for one, being able to tell your story is a great way to make a first impression and get whoever you're speaking to engaged through everything we discussed in the last chapter. This is an awesome way to get some small talk going which is another thing folks tend to have angst around.

Small Talk

I like to call small talk "productive conversations" because as you speak to somebody, you might not just be talking about the color of the sky or the weather. For me, those are a little lame. Sometimes, people are just used to it, and depending on the time of year, it may be appropriate to talk about the weather, especially if it was harsh as you were traveling to the event.

Great conversation starters, however, are around, 1) how long they've been in the industry/at the company, 2) your families: if people have children or pets since folks love to talk about their pets as if they are children, 3) hobbies that you may have like pottery or if you're taking some type of CrossFit class or if you love to cook or if you like to travel; others may include: books you are reading, movies that just came out, sports, other organizations you're involved with, etc.; all these things are great to talk about. These are things that people tend to gravitate toward because it's stuff that they know or may be passionate about, so it's easier to break the ice that way versus just making meaningless conversation.

If it's somebody who you've been trying to get in contact with, whether it's a potential manager or a potential mentor, it's great to get to know people on a personal level and connect that way because then they'll remember you. If they remember you, then they'll have a good feeling about you whenever the time comes to start discussing business.

If you just go straight in with the: 'hey, I've been following you for a while, and I really just want to know about x y z,' the person could be put off. Depending on the type of event you are at, they might not be trying to discuss business then, but are willing to connect with you on it later; so you need to read the room and just start as a human.

Handshake

Another great way to make a good first impression, which is something that I judge people on because I used to train folks in this category, is your handshake. Obviously, with COVID, people are a lot more cognizant of if they're touching each other or not, but for the folks who still need a little bit of human contact and just can't help themselves from sticking a hand out, your handshake needs to say I am here and I am confident.

If I grab your hand and it's a limp handshake, or your hand is super clammy, or you're trying to squeeze the life out of my hand, or you're trying to force me into a little princess handshake, I'm already feeling some type of way. If you come in with a nice strong, firm grip but nothing overpowering, then I get a good sense about you because you're confident in yourself enough to have a firm handshake and not insecure enough to feel like you have to squeeze my hand to have some dominance.

This may sound silly, but people pay to learn how to give handshakes. This is a part of training all around the globe, so having a great handshake is one thing that'll just set you further apart from other candidates.

I recently was at an event, and being a woman, men usually assume you're going to do the dainty princess-like handshake. I'm not here for people to kiss my hand; it just comes off as pretentious and ridiculous. So when I grabbed his hand and gave it a firm squeeze, he was caught off guard and ended up being the one to have the princess shake. He then apologized and re-shook my hand with a firmer grip, and we had a full discussion around it, and I could tell he had respect for me on a different level just from that brief interaction. People will remember you by your handshake.

Regardless of the environment or the reason you're meeting, whether in person, virtually, formal, or informal, it all starts with being a human, being relatable, and being yourself. If you're trying too hard to impress somebody, they will see right through it. If you're just trying to regurgitate a bunch of facts, they'll feel like you're not authentic and will be off-put most likely. However, if you're approaching somebody from a good place of just really trying to get to know them and telling them a little bit about yourself, who you are, and the things that you value and have passions around, ten times out of ten, the conversation will go a lot more smoothly, and you'll be able to connect with them after that point.

Action Item

You always want to have an ask at the end of your conversations with people with whom you want to develop a relationship. Go in first with the informal things of getting to know each other, have some conversation and laughs, connect and engage, and by the end, you can then have an ask of, "I would love to stay in contact; can I get your number/can I have your business card/can we set up a meeting to talk/can you put me in contact with so and so," or whatever the ask may be. The end of the interaction would be the prime time to do it. And you've already built rapport with the person, so they don't feel like you're just trying to use them. Sometimes it'll work even in the middle of a conversation, depending on what you're talking about.

Another great thing to do is to make sure that you are bringing value to the table as well, and we can get more into these two topics when we're discussing your network being your net worth.

Informational Interviews

This is having an informal conversation with someone to learn more about their position, the industry, their experiences, etc.

You aren't interviewing for any roles, but you are connecting with someone in the company of your interest or industry. You are "informally" interviewing them to find out more information that will help you get a leg up in your job search or information that will help you decide what to do next. Or you'll find out whether or not you want to move forward with pursuing a specific role or company.

These will normally occur once you've been introduced to someone who is out of your network (which we'll discuss in a later chapter). Having an action item in these conversations is highly important to take you to that next step in the process.

CHAPTER 8

Refreshing Your Biz Docs

The next step is having your documents together because when you go to these events, depending on what you're doing, you might want to have something in hand that you can hand off to people as they're speaking to you. It's important especially if it's a career fair or some type of business networking event where people might want to see something if it's pertaining to you getting a contract or a job. In this new day and age of technology, many people are walking around with QR codes to their platforms. So if this is you, make sure the link you are directing them to is professional and everything is in order, whether it's for your social media, website, portfolio, etc.

You also want to make sure digitally that you are in tip-top shape like with your LinkedIn. A lot of times, when you're sitting in the room, folks will go on LinkedIn and search the people who are around them. If you're talking to each other, more likely than not, after they get your name, they're going to look you up and scope your page. I've gotten speaking engagements through LinkedIn, and clients have also found me there. Plenty of people are getting their jobs through LinkedIn. LinkedIn is the platform to network with people, and 80% of jobs are filled through networking - not through conventional applying to job boards. Believe it or not, about 85% of jobs aren't even posted externally.

Social Media

If you are a working professional in a traditional job, I'd say just have all of your media private. Companies tend to look you up, especially on Facebook, when you're being vetted. I'd also steer clear of friending people who work in your company. I've seen many people get fired for things they've put on their Facebook or have repercussions because of a post.

Folks like to get political, and when you work for a company, they want your views to align with theirs or to be neutral. Even though it may seem unfair, your views can be taken as the company's views. If they are extreme, it definitely won't bode well for you. So just keep your stuff private and don't befriend your coworkers or bosses.

LinkedIn

Next is LinkedIn - the Facebook for professionals.

Your profile here is similar to a resume, but you can be a little more lax and personable. Always fill out your "about" section because it allows potential employers, clients, and folks in general to learn more about your journey. This can be a little bit of your "Tell me about yourself" mixed with key skills or strengths that you want to highlight from your career or areas you are trying to pursue.

For your experience, LinkedIn will order everything for you based on the year you worked at the company. You don't have to list everything in bullet point form like your resume. You can do short summaries of the impactful work that you did within each experience.

You'll want to make sure that your headline is impactful as well. My headline is basically my brand statement and what people can expect from me, "Career Coach |Recruiter | Talent Acquisition & Development | Speaker | Author | Fitness" or something to that effect.

LinkedIn is living and breathing. It's a platform, just like the rest of your media, that you want to stay active on to show people what you're up to. They may or may not engage, but eventually, folks will hit you up and say in passing that they see all the great things you are up to and to keep at it! They'll also let you know about any opportunities in their companies or people that they know if you post that you are looking for a job.

It's a great place to repost articles or things that others have posted and add a comment or two of your own in the post box. You can join different groups, sign up for various learning workshops and certifications, get access to articles on career tips, etc. Remember that it is more on the professional side than Instagram and YouTube, so again, you might be mindful of some of your posts. However, many people are breaking out of the stuffy mode (which I'm glad about) and sharing more personable things and showing more of their stances on social issues.

Whichever platform you choose, know your audience, research, and ensure that your brand and content align.

The Resume

Since you are working nine-to-five or something to that capacity, because a nine-to-five is never really a nine-to-five, let's walk through what your resume should look like when you're deciding that it's time to apply to a new role: whether or not it's internal for a promotion, external for a career change, or re-entering the workforce.

Resumes are another thing that can make or break people. So many of us were not taught correctly how to put a resume together. So many people have resumes that do not speak at all to their skills and, in my opinion, are completely atrocious which may or may not be any fault of their own. Resumes can be the first line of defense, depending on how you go about recruiting. You'll have about 7-10 seconds to impress the recruiter before they decide to toss you into the trash or move you to the next pile.

So as a previous HR business partner, and somebody who used to train folks on this, I want to give you the tea and help you out in your career so that you won't have to keep paying people to do your resumes and LinkedIn and whatever other documents. Having the knowledge is key, and applying it is the game-changer. So don't always pay somebody else to do something for you that you can do for yourself if it's something that can easily be in your wheelhouse. Now, if you got it like that and you just don't care, by all means, pay folks like myself to get your resume, your cover letter, and your LinkedIn together. You also want to weigh if it's worth your time and effort versus money. But unless it's something that's really time-consuming and an area that isn't your strength, I'd suggest saving the money and learning how to craft a great resume or at least knowing how to do so. It'll only help you, in the long run, to speak to those same points later during your interviews or networking events. And no one can capture your experiences the way you can. You just have to learn how to state it in a way that articulates your value.

Things to Consider:

Here are some basic rules of thumb to ensure your resume doesn't go into the trash as soon as the recruiter gets it.

First things first:

It need not be more than one page long. This can be one of those things that are nuanced based on the industry you're going into, but for the most part, you only need a one-pager. Anything more than this will most likely get you thrown in the trash because you should be able to concisely say what you need in one page. If you have to go past one page, that means you're not great at discerning what important skills and roles you've had that are relevant to the job you're applying to currently. This is not the same as a CV (usually in academia) which will most likely be more than one page.

You always want to make sure that you are highlighting things that correlate directly to the role or industry in which you are trying to break in. So if I'm going to apply to an HR role, I don't need to have things on my resume about when I worked in a paint shop if those skill sets don't directly translate over. If I was painting walls or just organizing colors or something of that nature, I don't need any of that on my resume for this job. However, if I did the hiring for the shop, helped create and implement a strategy for the company, then those skills can translate if I'm applying to a recruiting or business partner role.

Make sure you understand the role description or basic capabilities needed for whatever role or industry you are applying to. The worst thing you can do is submit a resume or document that has nothing to do with the job at hand because it will go directly into the trash. It will show that you are just sending out blanket applications and don't have a true interest in the company or role.

As a recruiter, we look for the slightest things to get rid of a candidate because a lot of times, depending on the role and company, you can have hundreds of applications. And we need to dwindle down the pile; you make it easy for us when you make basic or uninformed mistakes.

The next thing is to ensure that your formatting is appealing to the eye. Now, I don't mean this in a way that includes a bunch of colors and crazy fonts and all those things. Do not do that!

Use fonts like Times New Roman, Calibri Light, or Arial. Anything else is dicey. Your margins can be 1" left and ¾" for the rest.

Many companies are utilizing applicant tracking systems (ATS), and you want to make it easy for the software to read your resume. And even outside of that, you want it to be easy for the recruiter to read. This is because we spend about seven to ten seconds scanning your resume before deciding if you're going into the yes, no, or maybe pile. And you don't want to be scanned within the first two seconds and get tossed into the trash. So when I say formatting, I mean making sure that your headers look consistent, that your margins are good (using what's listed above), that your font is succinct, that your dates match correctly, and that the outline of your resume matches and is clear and concise. Below, I've inserted examples of what the formatting I prefer are because they're the most professional, in my opinion, and career placement firms as well as top 20 business schools utilize them. It's what Fortune 500 companies are used to seeing from the MBA applicants who are looked at, so to speak, as the cream of the crop.

Here are a few free resources to check formatting that other coaches and recruiters in my network utilize to test resumes through ATS software:

- JobScan (only get so many free scans a month)
- Resunate
- ResumeWorded

Along with formatting goes your sections, which you only really need three. You'll have your Education, Experience, and Additional - I'll go into detail about what should be listed under each.

Sample Resume 1: (For more recent graduates)

At the very top, your name should be in all caps and bolded, no bigger than size 14 (everything else will be size 11, except your headers which will be size 12). Directly underneath that should be, at the very least, your cell phone number and email. Some people put their address or the city and state they live in. If you aren't comfortable having your address there, don't put it. For your email, it needs to be professional. Don't have lilhotmama5@hotmail.com as your email on your professional resume. It may give your interviewer a good laugh, and then you're going straight into the trash. Do not have your mother, brother, or anybody else's contact information on your resume besides your own. When they're going to call you to get in contact about your interview or whatever else is going on, and your mom answers the phone - better believe you're probably going in the trash after that point. No one wants to chase you down. You're just making the process harder for the recruiter, and the harder you make it, the less likely you are to be hired.

So have all of your own information on there. And make sure that it's appropriate. It might sound simple, but you will not believe the emails I have seen on the resumes I've thrown away. And people do not want to hunt you down because you've put someone else's contact information. These things happen, and that is why I am warning not to do them. The resume has the contact info separated, but I would put them all on one line with '|' to separate your number from your email from your city, state.

The first section under that will be your education (if you're following sample resume one); this version is better if you recently graduated from a master's, PhD., undergrad, etc. program; you always want to make sure you list things in non-chronological order in each section. So your most recent schooling or jobs will go first for each section. This means wherever you're going to school currently, if you're in a grad program or undergrad, and you're about to apply for a role, list that and make sure you have the graduation date (the month and the year) that you expect to graduate directly across from it.

You should italicize your concentration right underneath your school name. You should bullet point any memberships for organizations or clubs that you either were a leader or a member of, as well as any fellowships that you may have received, especially for grad students.

Example:

EDUCATION

Spelman College, Atlanta, GA   May 2014
Bachelor of Arts Degree in Spanish, Cum Laude
- President, Sigma Gamma Rho Sorority, Inc., Epsilon Eta Chapter
- Council on International Education Exchange Fellow, Buenos Aires, Argentina

The experience section can contain paid and unpaid jobs that you have had or even roles that you held as a board member for whatever non-profit or organization you were part of. Again, list them in the order of your most recent first. If you have two jobs or were in two roles simultaneously, list the one you got last, first, and then the one that you had before that right after. I'll put an example below in case you're confused. You want to make sure that your bullet points are clear and concise, but I will get to that momentarily because that is the meat and potatoes (or impossible meat for my vegan folks) of your resume; that needs to be done correctly, or you will definitely not get the job.

EXPERIENCE

The Recruit Refinery LLC, Atlanta, GA   January 2020 - Present
Founder and Chief Talent Development Officer
- one liner
- one liner

Fun Company Co, Atlanta, GA   January 2019 - Present
HR Business Partner Associate
- one-liner
- one-liner

The last additional section will consist of any languages you speak proficiently or on an intermediate level. Don't list English if you are a native English speaker. You won't believe how many times I've seen that on people's resumes, and that's a no-brainer. Do not waste space on your resume with items that aren't relevant. It might land you in the trash. You can put any certifications that you have in this section, and you can put your interest in this section. You can also put volunteer activities in this section or any other skill sets that pertain to you, like Six Sigma or something of that nature.

Do not put basic skill sets like "customer service" or "basic Microsoft Office" because you should be able to describe your customer service skills within your experience in the bullet points above, and at this point in life with technology - everyone's expected to know basic Microsoft level skills on Word and Excel. If there are other software, though, that you are proficient with, like Workday, Salesforce, or something specialized in your industry, you can list those things out.

Next, when I say interests, I mean things like hobbies or things you are generally interested in. Now, this might sound unprofessional initially, and you might feel hesitant to put it on your resume, but this was advice I received from my mentor when I was applying to business school. I was skeptical but decided to trust him, and it made such a difference when I was applying to roles for my internships. Now I wholeheartedly pass this tip on to all of my clients. It can set you apart from other candidates and help you get the job, even if you may seem somewhat less qualified depending on the role. I say this because when you're interviewing with people or just speaking to them on a regular day, people love to talk about themselves, and they love to relate.

So if somebody sees that you like watching anime in your interests section, and they read all the mangas and watch the different shows, then they will be excited to have someone else to talk to about these things. People love to geek out, whether they admit it or not!

For example:

I have on my resume that I love writing novels. In the middle of one of my interviews with a panel, one of them asked me about the books that I was writing. And we spent a good five, maybe ten minutes talking about it. I told them I had started writing some when I was in elementary and middle school, gave them the synopsis of the stories, and how I'm in the middle of writing another book. They were so impressed by this and so interested in wondering if I would get them published or write sequels.

Another example I have is that I'm proficient in Spanish. At the time, I might have had the school I studied abroad at on my resume. One of my interviewers, again on a panel, stopped in the middle of the interview and tried to speak to me in Spanish, knowing this white man barely knew basic Spanish. However, I entreated him and responded, and we spoke for a line or two in Spanish before he said that's as good as it gets on his end.

Therefore, another lesson is to ensure you do not lie on your resume. If you write it on there, they will ask you about it. Do not make things up to sound smarter or more cultured or whatever thing may be going through your mind at that moment because you will be asked about it one way or another. It will most likely happen in your first interview since that's where they normally vet people around what's on their resume. But if not, please believe that the hiring manager or whoever else during another interview is going to ask some questions that you haven't been asked before pertaining to the experiences you listed on your resume. Don't lie.

What you can do is make sure your experience sounds highly impactful and results-driven. And there is a difference between doing that and straight up making things up and lying. If you write it down and can't speak to it, even if it's something close to what you've done, you've lost all credibility, and you've lost the job. So I will break down how to write a highly impactful bullet point on your resume and jazz up your experience so that it doesn't sound drab and boring.

Sample Resume 2: (Most widely used now)

FIRSTNAME LASTNAME

City, State | (555) 555-5555 | professional email | LinkedIn url (change text to reflect your name)

SUMMARY

Solutions-oriented __ professional with X years of experience. Proven record of skdjidj disojd is idjsodi dosji sdoisdji sidjsodij soidjsid sodijsid sidojsi cidou ja fast past-paced, innovative environments.

EXPERIENCE

WeSolve Issues, Los Angeles, California (*Startup*)   January 2022 - Present
Position Title (Contracted/Part Time - Remote)
- Analyze sdsjdisj soidsjdoijs odijsdoijs; dijsiofjd sdjfifjsiodjiosjdo sidjoisdjsipjds djgidjjsoijd sijdijs
- Source... idjsoidjsio dsoidjosidj sidjsofid soidjsodjs doisdjosi dsodijso dijsdoisd sjoisdjosijdio jsi

We Do Great Work Co, Atlanta, GA   January 2021 - March 2022
Founder, Chief Talent Development Officer
- Empowered 10+ clients ... doiosjdoisj dksmdosjdoi sjoidjsod sjdijajjoj d[sjdij[sijd[l sidjosj
- Partnered with empowerment organizations, guiding 40+ members to utilize their brands & professional skills to influence key stakeholders and create new career opportunities
- Utilized social media & CRM systems, to sell & market services & products to potential clients

CPG Inc, City, State   July 2019 – September 2020
HR Business Partner
- Staffed $2MM+ ....sdsdijso sdisspd[o osdpospod sodspdoi irojrioe psd posd
- Created & implemented .... Sjodijsojdi sodfsjdi o sdoi sdpsdp disjodijs psodfksp
- Collaborated with 6 functional leaders .... Idjosjo f sofdsfjsoi . dosjoij s dosjdi... soij
- Identified .... Dskjsoifj s. sdfodsijdojs o
- Partnered with .... Dskdfjk slkfsdjk sidsdjf... osdfijsodj .osjfsdoijs. sdfsjsjf .dfsfjsofjdosjdo.sf sofdiosjdos
- Utilized Workday ... dlsjdoisj d idovido sodis sosidf g pgopdg qeqioe idjsoidjis soidjosdi sj
- Cofounded dsiodsodj .Idsodjsio ..sdi osoij ... disjdoisdjos .sfgfid ijdoisjdoijso disjodijsi di
- Led ... dosdijosidj d sidsoduso sds disdo wkewco ow oioijf fewcowij dffpgi wepowpe fiofifdu kdmosidjs foifdfjdif weoijroijf goigfj]
Position Title 1, City, State   June 2018 – August 2018
- Forecasted ... Osjdoisjdoi sjdiojsoidj ijdoisjdoisjf siojdfisjodfjosijfdiji disjdoij sidjsoid si
- Founded sdsdj sdijsoidjsoij iojfpdfpo gpokgpofogpj wperowkek pdfoidpfok ;lekwpoekwpo

Company 4, Chicago, II.   May 2015 – June 2017
Position Title
- Coached 16 client supervisors across 9 Fortune 500 companies ... dsijdosij sdksodisj dsklndsoidj sodmsoidjsoi dsdoisdj soij disj i
- Trained..... sdijsoidj dkjsodjsid sdfk sodjsiodj sdkmsodijsodi skmdosidjso ds idosj idj
- Engineered .... Dsdijsodi sdijsoijdios sdijsoid sodj sdiosjdi sdo sjd sidjoisj fpokgpo kdgopgkd
- Partnered with ..... ijdosijdoi sodijsidosid sidjsidj si sdokspokd sopdkspdkpos dposkodk sdkoskpdksdk sokd
- Presented dsjdoisjdoi kdsmsdijsid ijidojajd sdkisjfdoisjdoifj sodfijsofij sdoijsiodjso disidj sdjid

EDUCATION

Name of University Program | M.B.A XYZ| Month/Year – Month/Year
College Name | B.A. Major| City, State | Month/Year - Month/Year

ADDITIONAL

Languages: Spanish - Intermediate/Proficient (speaking, reading, writing)
Skills: Workday, Boolean, Six Sigma Black Belt, Certified XYZ (2017); Advisory Board Member XYZ
Interests: hobbies, interests, fun facts (travel, anime, cooking, little league coaching, Pilates, etc.)

You'll notice that I didn't mention anything about having a career profile or career summary on resume sample one. If you aren't switching careers or re-entering the workforce, you shouldn't need one.

However, if you're pivoting to a new industry, are re-entering the workforce, or are pretty early in your career (recent college graduate), you can include one. That being said, don't make the recruiter feel they've wasted 20 seconds trying to decipher what "great" thing you want them to know about you when you could've written a bombastic one-liner. Instead, do a SHORT summary (like two lines long like the one listed in resume sample two), hitting the key skills you have that are important for that role or industry.

It's a very quick summary of highly impactful statements that will then be followed by examples of those within your experience bullet points. It's helpful to see it quickly if you are switching careers or re-entering the workforce to give quick credibility. You can also give a brief few words about the type of environment you've worked in or the ones you want to work in. I put "fast-paced and innovative" in the example above because most people will want you to be able to navigate those types of environments. If you have never worked in that type of environment, though, don't put that you have. You can say that you are looking to work in that type of environment moving forward, e.g., 'looking to work in a fast-paced, innovative space/environment.'

In general, utilize the space on your resume to speak about how you are an asset and the value you bring from what you've done previously. As a recruiter, I am looking to see what you can do for the company and me. I'm looking to see what skills you have that my team can utilize. I'm looking to see how you analyze things or what leadership capabilities you carry.

You'll notice that on resume sample two, the experience is right under the summary and that education is last. Many recruiters and companies are also starting to look for this type of formatting. Education isn't as important as it used to be and could cause bias if you didn't attend a top school. So including it toward the bottom will let the recruiter see your skills and experiences before knowing where you were educated with less judgment.

One more tidbit is to exclude putting a picture on your resume. It opens you up to discrimination and can just be unprofessional. Unless you're in the entertainment industry and going into modeling, where they need to see what you look like, which is still low-key discrimination because they contact you majorly based on your looks, then leave it off.

You can mix the two versions together for spacing purposes or to fit whatever your needs are. I have more of the sample two resume formats currently as I'm re-entering the workforce. Do what's best for you.

So now, let's get on to the good stuff.

One-Liners - the meat and potatoes.

Your one-liners, also known as your bullet points, should be concise and to the point. They describe what action you took and the results from that action.

A few watch-outs as we think about writing our one-liners:

Spelling and grammatical errors:

- Simple errors like this give recruiters a reason to toss you in the trash

Super long bullets:

- Each one should only be one to two lines long

Too many bullet points:

- Only have about three to four at most per experience
- You can get away with more for your most recent experience or if you don't have a lot of experience in general

Industry lingo and abbreviations:

- Most likely, the person reviewing your resume isn't in the function to which you're applying, so they won't know what the abbreviations or certain lingo will mean
- Write things out and speak in layman's terms (so a ten-year-old could understand)

Spacing:

Have enough white space on the page so it doesn't look cluttered but also not empty

When you're writing out your bullet points, they should start with an action word/verb. I will list a few action words below that are pretty good to use regardless of what industry you may be in.

Sample action words to start your one-liners:Analyzed

- Executed
- Collaborated
- Managed
- Implemented
- Organized
- Founded
- Created/Engineered

- Influenced
- Launched
- Evaluated
- Conducted
- Performed
- Developed
- Designed
- Identified

These are just to name a few, but there are many that can be utilized. You just want them to start off with a high impact. You can Google 'high impact action verbs for a resume' or 'resume action verbs' to get a full list.

You also want your one-liner to answer the question, "So what?" The answer to that will be the results. So to ensure your statement is high impact, you need to list what you did and why it was important. Otherwise, no one's going to care unless it shows some value, and that value can be translated into their company or the position at hand.

So let's say you worked at McDonald's and were a cashier. You don't want to write a basic statement that doesn't really convey the fact that you did something grand. Working as a cashier might not seem all that glorious, but it's all in how you portray it.

Let me give you a bad example of what to write on your resume:

"Worked as a cashier and took money from customers."

There's an action verb like we discussed, but it doesn't really describe what's going on and what impactful actions you took. Saying that you worked as a cashier doesn't really amount to much. Then saying that you took money from customers doesn't really serve any real impact because you're just stating what a cashier does. What result can you correlate to being a cashier taking money? Does this make sense?

So let's break it down further and create a statement with more value added and some skills and capabilities.

Improved statement:

"Managed financial transactions of a $1MM franchise, ensuring accurate bookkeeping and cash reserves for daily operations."

Now which of the two seems more valuable to a potential manager? Which one can you pull out some skills that can be transferable into your job? Which one actually shows some impact?

Obviously, the answer is the second example. We start with a strong action verb like 'managed' because you're letting people know you're good at overseeing things. Next, you're saying that you're managing financial transactions of a 'million-dollar franchise' which means you can deal with bigger budgets or handle operations under a bigger company. Next, you're giving the result that comes from managing those transactions, therefore answering the "so what?"

Yes, it sounds great that you can manage financial transactions, but why do I care? So what does that do for me? You're answering that by ensuring that bookkeeping is accurate, which is important for audits. You're also letting the interviewer or hiring manager know that you have attention to detail because you're looking for accuracy. You're also saying that you're making sure there's enough cash on hand for the daily operations, which means that you're planning out for the day and thinking ahead in the bigger picture. You also quantified some results here, which is also key to having highly impactful statements, which I'll discuss in a few paragraphs. There's more you can say with that, but these are just basic examples I'm giving.

Companies love to see how you can factor in what you're doing with the overarching strategy of the department or the organization, and this example shows that.

Do we see how this sounds way more professional, impactful, and appealing than just saying that you worked as a cashier and took money from people? These are the things you need to consider as you are writing out the bullet points for your resume. Keep in mind I didn't lie about what I was doing. I didn't make up something that was out of my wheelhouse. Because as a cashier, you are overseeing financial transactions for the company, you are making sure that the proper amount of money is accounted for to be able to run for the day, which in turn goes into having accurate books for the ledgers. So think hard and dig deep when you're making your one-liners. Truly think about the impact of what your day today has within the company.

To write this out, think about all the positions you've held; think about the day-to-day things you do; think about the projects you're on and the scope of them as well as the general strategies in place. Look at your role description; look at the skills that are needed for your job.

Use the list we wrote about earlier of the skills and capabilities you built in your different roles. This is why I had you write your accomplishments and strengths earlier so that you have something to pull from as you're writing your resume. You have a point of reference.

Now that you've done that, you can translate those things into one-liners. The next most important thing is the result that came from whatever actions you took within your job. Because again, this is what sells people on why you should get hired.

On the resume, after you give a synopsis of your action, put a comma and the next word after that should end in an '-ing.' Notice that I put 'ensuring' in the example above.

Not everybody uses this method, but as somebody who is going through your resume, it is the easiest way to pinpoint your results. Mixing it all throughout the one-liner will only cause confusion and make people think hard about what you're writing. You can also convey the same point using 'via' or 'through.' If you start with the result, "Forecasted $2MM product sales via creating xyz tracker system," you also give the so what. The harder you make somebody think when they're just trying to glance through, the more likely you'll be tossed into the trash. That may sound really ridiculous, but again we sift through hundreds of resumes depending on the project or role, and if you start to make things complicated, we're tossing you out. So always make it easy for the person reviewing your documents so that within a quick second, they understand what you do and the value add that you have.

Another point is that with your results (or even within the context), if you can quantify them - DO IT! I understand that not every position involves things that can be quantified, but it definitely helps if you can. Only do it if it makes sense. Don't quantify minuscule numbers just to try and sound good, either. Make sure the quantification makes sense.

Example:

"**Coached** 16 client supervisors to delegate challenging projects to new interns, *freeing* up 1200+ client hours."

I'm bolding the action words and underlining the different areas of quantification to show how it can go across both the result and context portion of the one-liner.

If I'm freeing up 1200+ hours for my clients, that's so much more time they can focus on more grueling projects and is attractive to anyone who manages a team. If you are having trouble coming up with quantifying what you do, ask your manager or someone on your team the best way to do so if possible.

You also want to think about how you write your title. You don't just want to write something basic like a bartender. It could be a mixologist or something that essentially equates to the same thing but sounds a little fancier. Titles like 'operation manager' or 'general manager' are okay because those are used across multiple industries. Hence, people have a pretty good idea of the type of work entailed when you have that listed.

I edited a client's resume utilizing all of these tips and tools, and he sent me an email stating that he had gotten a role as a general manager at a new lounge in Chicago in a very popular and pricey area. It was great because he had 20+ years of experience, with a few gaps between different roles, but wasn't sure exactly how to speak to everything.

This leads to a few takeaways you may struggle with as you put together your resumes.

Gaps:

Many people were laid off during the pandemic, so at this point, companies are more lenient and understanding around times when you weren't working. Even pre-COVID, recruiters had a more understanding mindset regarding people having gaps between roles. In order to help with this, you want to be able to speak to these things in your interview or when you are networking.

The best way is to keep it short and sweet to avoid detracting the rest of the conversation. Discuss what you learned during this time off: maybe you took a course, got a certification, etc. If you were at home taking care of a loved one, you could equate it to becoming the general manager of the household. You had to manage their schedule, improve your own time management, delegate responsibilities, take care of those added bills, etc., during this time.

There is always a way to positively spin a situation that someone could view as negative. Take a moment to reflect on what happened during this time, craft a short story of the skills you gained, and then navigate back to the interview by stating how you can use those new skills within the role.

I stated that my client had 20+ years of experience, but clearly, we didn't have 20 years jam-packed into one page. Therefore, do not go back past 7-10 years of experience on your resume. Anything more than that probably isn't relevant given changes in technology, laws, etc. Pick the experiences that make the most sense for that job and list those things on the resume. You will most likely have more than one resume, which is normal. Each can be tailored to different functions - one for HR, one for marketing, etc., or the different types of capabilities needed for said roles. If you are applying to a super relationship-based company, make sure you have examples of experiences where you were building and fostering relationships.

This also is where your brand comes back into play. Whatever your overarching core statement is, those things should come through in the different roles you've held and experiences you've had.

Because I develop talent, build relationships, and liberate mindsets, many of my experiences spoke to those things. When I was interviewing with people or conversing with them at an event, I spoke about those things.

Also, make sure you have a solid answer for why you are leaving your current company or deciding to re-enter the workforce. This is another thing that might trip people up when you start having phone screens or are getting into the interviewing stage of your recruiting process. We'll come back to this later.

CHAPTER 9

Is Your Network *Really* Your Net Worth?

We've all heard the age-old adage: your network is your net worth, but how true to form is that?

It depends on you at the end of the day because what you do with your network makes the difference.

You could have a millionaire in your network, even one to two degrees of separation from you, and it would mean nothing if you didn't take the time to build out that relationship. It's just like having a car but you still walk everywhere; it can get you to where you need to go quicker, but you're not utilizing it at all, so you're still struggling or doing things unnecessarily the hard way.

So the most important thing I'll say for you is to make sure that you cultivate your relationships and know which relationships cater to certain areas of your life or certain goals that you may have. Everyone isn't equipped to deal with everything that you have going on.

If you're trying to go into marketing, don't talk to the engineer about the best way to climb that path.

There are two main types of networks that you can have. The first is your IN-network people, and the second is your OUT-of-network people.

In-Network:

In-network people are the folks you know firsthand and have met or have some type of relationship with already. So you can consider these people your friends, mentors, coaches, classmates and alumni from your school, old professors, your manager or other people on your team at work, folks you've met and exchanged information with from different organizations you may be a part of, and things of that nature.

These are the people who, if you call them, have some idea of who you are and won't be caught off guard because you're some rando.

These relationships are highly important to make sure that you cultivate. You may not realize when you need advice, coaching, or guidance from somebody who's already in your network at some point later down the line.

For example:

If you're not currently interested in going into product management, but your mentor on the job also happens to be a product manager, then in a couple of years, when you decide to go into product management, that would be somebody who you could hit up to get some type of direction about product management. Having that in-network person allows you to benefit from the relationship's longevity. It doesn't matter whether they point you to other people or give you a foundation to start from; it's better than 'square none'.

On the downside, if you leave that job, and you aren't keeping in contact with this person, meaning you aren't meeting with them quarterly or checking in every however many months, and you just let the relationship go to the wayside, chances are it'll be weird when you hit them up out of the blue about that role depending on the relationship you had when you worked together. If you got along well while you worked, and a few years go by, and you hit them up, they might not have an issue.

This happened to me when I reached out to folks on LinkedIn about different tech companies they were at to gauge their experiences. A woman who had left the nonprofit I worked at 5+ years ago is working at Tesla and I reached out to her recently to discuss her time there, and she was more than happy to hear from me. We were cool when we worked together and would eat lunch together at times.

As a general rule of thumb, make sure you touch base with people even if you're not interacting directly with each other anymore. Even if that means liking or commenting on a post on social media. You never know when you might need them, or they might need you. This is key because no one wants to feel like they're being used or that a relationship is not reciprocal.

Your in-network people are also great because if an opportunity arises on their end, and they know you're interested and are privy to your capabilities, they can put in a good word for you. They can also help you build the skill sets you need to attain whatever goal you've set for yourself. So if you're new to product management, having someone who can show you the ropes, put you in contact with the right people, or tell you what groups to join so that you can expand your network will be awesome.

The same goes for if there is a position that you want to apply for in a separate department from your own, and you know a manager that works in that department and have a great relationship with them. They can then put in a good word for you when an opportunity presents itself. They could also help you figure out what path you need to take to get into that position based on your current skills and capabilities so that you can work to be exactly where you need to be in order to secure the job.

I want to stress that you should make sure your relationships are reciprocal. You don't want to be that person seen with their hand always out, asking for or needing stuff, but you're never providing any value to the situation. It needs to be an exchange of value even if it's not equivalent, especially if it's somebody who's perceived to be in a higher position than you are. They understand that you may not have as much to offer, but since you want to offer something or support them in some way, it shows your willingness to meet them halfway. Sometimes people don't need physical things; they might just need someone to support and spread the word about what they are doing.

I've used this countless times, even with the mentor I mentioned earlier who helped me get into business school that I met through my job. I was drawn to him because he was Black, had business ownership, and was in a place financially that I was aiming for. We met once a month, and he helped me through that process. Every time we met up, I'd always ask if there was anything I could do for him. More recently, we've gotten back in touch, and I usually check in with him at least once or twice a year since I don't live in Chicago anymore, and we don't meet face-to-face. He recently introduced me to a friend; he gave me some things I could do to help him around business items that he had going on - whether it was feedback about content or liking a Facebook page or things of that nature. I also have another mentor who has a podcast they wanted me to listen to about Black entrepreneurs and give feedback or refer people to be featured. You always want to ensure you are also being of service and not just needing something anytime you speak with people. A "give me, give me, give me" mindset turns people off even if you had a good relationship before that.

I have another mentor I gained after business school by attending an alumni event for the Consortium, and she's a career coach. This was when I was thinking about coaching, not necessarily all in on it because I was going to work in corporate. But I knew one day I wanted to get into coaching, and I liked her style. I reached out to her for mentorship, and she helped me figure out a program to get my certification for career coaching. From my end, she would send me content to get feedback to see if it was helpful or to fill out forms, listen to podcasts, or share an article. You want to ensure that you are doing these things, checking in, and making sure that they are okay. Don't just try to lean on them to make sure that you're okay, because they have lives too, their own issues, struggles, and goals.

Connecting them to other people is one way you can really be of service to somebody if you don't have anything physical to offer. That is always a plus. People are always looking to grow their network, and if you have someone who can truly be of value to them or they can be of value to one another, that goes a long way as well. Be on the lookout when you're out speaking with folks and learning about what they do, and see if you can connect them to someone you know, especially if they've expressed that they want or need more people within this realm.

If there are people in your network that you haven't spoken to in a while but truly did value their relationship, make it a point to start reaching back out to them again and rebuilding that relationship. Again, you don't want to show up out of the blue with your hand out when you haven't spoken in a significant amount of time. Just touching bases with them, even if it's twice a year, is still better than no communication. You always want to talk to people before you need them for something. Remember that.

Out-of-Network (OON)

As for your out-of-network folks, these are people that you aren't directly tied to, so there's some degree of separation there, or you don't know them at all. If your mentor has a colleague that could do you a favor or they think would be great for you all to speak, that is somebody who's out of your network.

Recall the example that I gave of my mentor introducing me to one of his friends who was in somewhat of a similar space: somebody who was out of my network who I was able to connect with, and that also was an informational interview.

OONs are also people who you initially meet at different events, exchange information with, and build relationships with through small talk (or productive conversations) when you first meet them to learn more about them and for them to learn more about you. Then you can decide at that moment if you feel like developing a relationship with them or if it's in neither of your best interests to build on it.

I would always follow up with your new network after meeting and give a brief synopsis of the conversation that you had so that they remember who you are specifically because they've probably talked to tons of people by the end of that occasion. We don't tend to have the best memories, especially if a lot is going on. Make it easier on them to remember who you are.

I would also compliment them around something that they spoke about or their work because flattery isn't a bad thing as long as it's coming from a good place. It usually gets you in people's good graces. I'd also have that action item for them, especially if you plan on developing this relationship.

This is what you would call a "call to action" (CTA). As we discussed earlier, let them know what it is that you're looking to do and ask them to connect you with someone or set up a coffee chat with them. Let them know you are looking to continue this relationship. Also, ask if there is anything you can do to support them so that they know you are willing to be of value in the relationship you're building. That will always bode well, even if they say no. Having the confidence to ask for what you want while simultaneously offering yourself as a service speaks volumes because it shows that you're not just being selfish.

Oftentimes, there are always those days when people will reach out and ask you for something, even when not initially.

So given the previous chapter where we discussed what networking is in general and now the different types of networking, **it is your homework to:**

- List out the ways that you can meet new people to add to your network based on your goals within your corporate career
- Determine what types of people it would behoove you to have in your corner
- Qualify and quantify the value you can bring to people? Is this a realistic value?

If you don't have the resources, don't go offering and overleveraging yourself, as that could put you in a bad situation. Set realistic expectations, and don't set yourself up for failure. You don't want to over-commit to something and then lose somebody's trust. The best thing you can do is be authentically you at every stage of your journey.

Also, start thinking about people who aren't in your network, how you can connect with them, and what events and avenues you can take to do so. Is there somebody that's in your network that's connected to someone that's out of your network? Think about that.

Is there a space you're trying to get into that you don't know anyone there right now? If so, you might need to join different organizations or meet-up groups or cold reach out to folks on LinkedIn.

This is called getting into the right environments. This is pivotal to the growth of your career. Environment can be the number one killer of people's goals and dreams. We discussed in chapter one that you need to be around the right people for your mindset, but this also goes for your trajectory in life. When you are setting yourself in environments that are conducive to expanding your mind and perception of what you believe to be possible, you will find yourself doing things you didn't think imaginable that are bringing you closer to realizing your dreams.

If you are putting yourself in environments where people are continuously achieving things in their careers that you may have felt were only possible for a select few, then it will open your mind to the things that you can do in your career as well. You will be more inclined to start taking action to fast-track your career path. You will connect with people who can propel you further than if you were trying to thug it out on your own.

You will find yourself connecting with people who have gone through the struggle and have made it to the other side. You will connect to people who can help you put the right systems in place or figure out the next move that will position you for that promotion. You will begin to find people who are more about collaborating and sharing resources than those who have a scarcity mindset and might not be as willing to help you because they feel that only one of you can make it to the top. Avoid these types of negative people and environments. Continuously find the environments and people who will challenge you to get uncomfortable and push yourself beyond what you thought possible. These environments are virtual and in person.

So, think about the different ways you can network in person and virtually in these types of environments. Social media has allowed us to build virtually and build strong relationships without ever having to physically meet people. So build those relationships and remember that you want to be talking to people before you need them. You don't only want to reach out to somebody when you actually have a favor to ask of them. Reach out to them before then.

CHAPTER 10

Let's Get Ready to Netwoooork!

Yay, now it's time for the fun part! Practicing networking, woohoo! Since you've shifted your mindset about it being something negative into being a great aspect of your career development, we are going to put the things we spoke about into play.

As usual, this chapter will build off the stuff that we did in the previous chapters. That being said, you are going to start identifying people that you *need* to network with or want to network with. These will be people who are both in your network and out of your network.

Step 1:

The way this is going to work is that each week for the next six weeks, you should list two people in your network and two people out of your network that you want to connect with. Reach out to them (this can also be the type of people you want to network with as it pertains to out of network folks you don't know, e.g., the director of the marketing department, someone in the tech industry, etc.). That can look like you emailing them, setting up coffee chats with them, having a phone call, etc. It counts as long as you are contacting them, checking in and building that rapport.

Also, make it a point to attend an event or two bi-weekly to meet new people.

Reach out to folks for six weeks and attend at least two to three events over the month to expand your network and deepen current relationships.

Step 2:

Note how each interaction happens, whether you're having a coffee chat with somebody or going to a local event down the street. Also, keep tabs on the difference that it's making within your work.

Do you feel refreshed?

Are you feeling more positive about moving forward in your career?

Are you excited to connect with people?

Do you have your call to action ready and the way that you can be of value in the relationship on deck?

Truly take note and write down how this impacts you and where you want to be. People seem appreciative when you're following up with them, checking in on them, and bringing up things from previous conversations, whether it be about their family or something they're doing within their work.

Are they excited that you're offering to support them in any type of way, and have you supported anyone since beginning this?

Step 3:

After taking notes and writing down your interactions, <u>reflect</u> and see what went well and where opportunities lie to improve. Do this at the end of each week so that the next week you can be stronger and more confident. At the end of the month or two, look back over your notes and notice the growth you've had amongst any differences between your weeks. If people give you feedback, make a note of that as well.

This chapter is simple but quite effective because if you implement it, it'll make a difference in how you approach networking, how you view your relationships with people, and how they view their relationships with you. This is truly where your brand starts to show through and where you can practice your "tell me about yourself," share your story, and emphasize your value add.

People know me as the "networker" in my corporate realm and realm of entrepreneurship. I'm always at an event and inviting people out to places or connecting folks in my network together. People have started coming to me about getting connected to the events I attend, commenting on my posts about how I'm always somewhere, or making statements in person about how I'm always networking and they need to get like me. Check out my Instagram page @iamkbepps to see Nehemiah Davis (Neo – Black multimillionaire entrepreneur) tell the crowd at his pop-up event how I have the characteristics of a winner because I'm always in the room and making myself known. People notice and take note, and I want the same for you.

Once people know enough about you, the things that you value, and your strengths and experiences, they can better recommend you to roles as they become open and know that you too can be of service to them.

This is a great example of what just happened to me recently. I've decided to accept a management role at a Black startup company under Combs Enterprises. The CEO of the company is a Spelman Alumna, and the only way I found out about the position is because of our Spelhouse chat on GroupMe. She posted the position and one of my friends tagged me because they knew I'd be a perfect fit given my background in HR and business strategy.

Of course, graduating from the same alma mater among having the right qualifications only worked more in my favor! Not only will I be contributing to the growth of a Black-owned business that will be providing resources and wealth opportunities to other Black businesses, but I will also be exposed to more opportunities and a broader network of folks that will only help me down the line in my own career.

All these things tie together. So be sure that you are solid in your story or that you're at least practicing it with people in your network currently: like your family, friends, maybe some colleagues and trusted individuals. This is vital so that when you are networking and talking to these heavy hitters who could make a big difference for you, you aren't fumbling around on your words, and you aren't stuttering around when they're asking about different experiences that you've had.

Make sure you're confident and well-versed in your story around what you bring to the table, what you value, and what you want. Even if you're at a point where you're still figuring it out, you can very well speak to everything that's happened to you up until this point, and you can give some type of idea of what you're leaning toward moving forward. That could be your ask - that they help you figure it out based on x y and z but in this case, you will still need to have that foundation to build on.

Don't sleep on LinkedIn as a place to network; that's how I got one of my speaking engagements and a contractor role as a career coach for a different start-up. Again as I said before, connections on LinkedIn also count to get you a degree of separation closer to someone who can help you. The only way they found me was through one of my connections celebrating and commenting on a post I had. Then that organization went through my page and website, liked what they saw, and reached out to me to speak to their cohort of women about building their brand and utilizing that to move forward in their careers. I also cold-reached out to recruiters on LinkedIn to learn more about their experiences at companies I'd consider working at within that function.

Lastly, I'll give one last example more so from my real estate interest. As I alluded to earlier, I was going out weekly to events. I met so many people in such a short time that I was sitting at the table with millionaires and billionaires within two to three weeks of really going heavy on that path. I reconnected with one of my friends from graduate school and found so many new like-minded individuals that I didn't even realize possible. I was exposed to a different scene of people in the same city I had been living in for years.

So when I tell you that your *mindset shift* plays a large role in how you carry yourself moving forward and attracting the forces that you want and need, there's no lie!

Small Warning:

Don't underestimate the degrees of separation when you are networking. They can work for or against you depending on your attitude. You never know who knows who, so watch what you say and don't talk badly about anyone. You could destroy a relationship before it's even made.

An example of this is when I was in business school, and we were at this huge Orientation Program for all the folks who were Consortium fellows. Everyone in our graduating class from the multiple schools was in a huge group chat on GroupMe. It was the day of interviews, and some people in the group were talking trash about the interviewers and some of the interviews they had. Other folks were separately going back and reaching out to those interviewers because they were previous colleagues or folks they knew from before business school, which killed the chances of the other people getting into those roles or having any chance to get in good with that company. So stay professional. Don't be messy; bring something to the table, and ensure that the other people are also bringing value to you.

So go forth and have fun networking in these streets!

CHAPTER 11

Speaking Like a Boss

Now it's time to show that all your hard work has paid off. This means the interview!

You want to utilize this to your advantage to figure out not only if they want to hire you but if the company is a fit for you culturally, personally, and developmentally... all the things.

This is not only their time to test you and feel you out but the time for you to feel them out and see if they are aligned with your values and are about their business. That way, when you get the offer, you can make a clear decision because you have all the information you need, not make a decision out of desperation.

The first step is to reflect on the last time you interviewed, whether it was a preliminary phone screen, virtual, or in person.

Think about all the things that went well, and think about all the areas of improvement. For those things that went well, make sure that you capitalize on them and practice keeping those things when speaking to somebody. For the areas of improvement, make a note of them, be aware of them as you are practicing, and have others who are helping you point them out.

There are multiple ways to interview or interact with somebody as you're doing so. It can be virtual, pre-recorded, or in-person.

Virtual

Virtual is live, real-time with a panel of people or one person on your computer through Zoom, Teams, or any other software people use to make conference calls. If there is more than one person on the call, you need to make sure you are acknowledging everyone.

Sometimes there may be one person who is speaking more than the other, but don't let this throw you off. You still should address everyone accordingly, whether it's in the beginning, throughout the interview as you're giving your answers, and also at the end when you're asking questions or saying your goodbyes and thank yous.

Pre-recorded

For recorded interviews, normally, you log into a software that the company sends you, and they have pre-outlined questions that you are to answer. Sometimes you get more than one opportunity to record your answer; other times, they give you a time limit, and you only have one chance to record. So that is why it's vital to practice, practice, and practice ahead of time so that you don't get caught off guard and panic because of the time limitations.

In-person

Last is in person, which is obviously live, and it's more interpersonal. It has the same components as virtual to a degree, but this time, you get to sit face to face with someone. There's more of an opportunity to read the room. You can interact better and physically shake hands and things if permitted in the world of COVID, and you can get a better feel for how they're reacting to your answers and can feed off of each other's energy. Now the energy factor may have to come full-throttle on your end because sometimes interviewers can seem intimidating. At times this is on purpose; other times, it's just because that's their personality, and you can't let that shake you. You need to come in positive with high energy, but not super high energy where you're disrupting what's going on/over the top, but being: confident, passionate, happy, and yourself.

Basic to-do's:

Company Research/Hiring Manager Research:

It is best to look up whoever your interviewer is on LinkedIn if possible. Find out about their background, see if you have anything in common, and learn about their journey of how they got to where they are currently so that you have talking points either during your introductions or at the end when you're asking questions. You'll also be able to see if they took a similar route to what you want to do, and you can have more insight on maybe issues they've had in their journey or things that were helpful for them as they were on this career path.

It's also best to do your due diligence by looking up details on the company that you're going to be involved with, the role you're applying for, and what it truly entails, as well as the type of community that the organization serves if social responsibility is important (or you're in nonprofit).

I will give a few brief things to utilize in this process:

Ways to research your company are to look through annual reports, listen to quarterly calls if they are available to the public, and look through their 10K report if it's a publicly owned company because that lists everything that you need to know about the company: from financial situations to the products that they have, to where they are located globally, to any joint ventures they may have, etc. The 10k literally has everything you want or need to know about the company.

You can also talk to people who work in those areas to get inside information on cultural things that are going on, recent issues that they may be dealing with, or some great things that they have coming down the pipeline if they can share that information publicly. Setting up Yahoo or Google alerts for that company can also help.

The last thing you want to do is try to work for a company that you know nothing about, or that is involved in something that is against your morals or values. So it's great to do your research to know what they are about, what they are involved in, the services they offer, and who their end consumers are.

You will also need to be yourself. There is nothing worse than sitting in an interview with somebody who is trying to impress you or someone who is just saying a bunch of fluff to try to win you over. Think of it as going out on a date. Would you want to date somebody who's just trying to get over on you and tell you all the things they think you want to hear so they can get to that second date? Or would you prefer to get to know someone who's being themselves, even if they are a little bit nervous, but you can tell that they are genuine and truly have the best intentions and are willing to put in the work for the right reasons?

Interviewing is dealing with human interaction and connecting yourself with someone or another entity you want to be aligned with and feel is a fit. It is okay to have a good time while you interview. Just make sure to keep whatever professionalism about you so as not to detract from the purpose of why you're there.

When I tend to have interviews, we usually end up having a decent chat and are laughing and relating to one another in some form or fashion.

My most recent interview, I connected on the fact that we both traveled to Ghana, were both in sororities, and of course that we both went to Spelman. She had sifted through all my information on LinkedIn, my resume, etc. and was super excited about the work I had done which added to the pleasantries of our conversation.

During a business school career fair, I left one of my interviews after having a great conversation and some laughs with the interviewer, and one of my classmates was sitting outside. They told me that they didn't even want to go into the room after me because they had never laughed or had a great time during an interview like that. It makes a big difference. Don't be so nervous and uptight that you miss that moment to build some rapport.

Dress code:

Make sure that you are appropriately dressed, even if it is virtual. You never know what is going to happen. You may have to jump up quickly because something is going on. If you're only dressed nicely from the torso up and yet only have your undies on or pajama bottoms from the waist down, then you're on the road to embarrassment. You'll be remembered for not a good reason even though you may have supplied them with some good laughs for the day. For my ladies, you don't want to wear a too revealing top because you don't want to detract from them seeing your value as an employee. And it's not just men who may be looking at you. Even women get distracted and can be wondering why you're dressed with your cleavage out and find it inappropriate as well.

You also don't want to wear clothes that are too tight-fitting for the same reason or skirts and dresses that are too short. For the love of all things great, please do not go in there with 7-inch stilettos because you'll also draw attention to yourself in the wrong manner. You also want to be able to walk in your shoes without looking like Bambi going down the hallway. A nice two to three-inch pump is fine. Make it closed-toed to add more of that professional touch. But whatever industry you are going into, just make sure you're doing your research. If you're going into tech and people tend to dress more casual, like in jeans and polo, then make sure you know that instead of showing up in a suit and tie.

I'm not in the tech space, so I will not advise on what they deem as appropriate wear, but I will say again to do your research. For most spaces, dressing professionally in a button-down shirt, some slacks, and closed-toed shoes for men is the norm. A nice Polo and slacks or khakis can also work as well, depending. For my guys, make sure that your suit jackets fit if you have one on. If you aren't wearing one, please have on a tie and make sure it's not a baby tie or super skinny tie. If you sweat through your shirts, it's probably better to have on a jacket or those little sweat pads under your arms so that you don't feel embarrassed or any more nervous. You don't want your pants to be super huge like how we used to dress in the '90s. You know how the Black men would walk around in those "preacher" suits that were oversized and looking crazy. Don't do that. It's not attractive, and folks will laugh at you. Tailor your suits if you can or get them as close-fitting to normal as possible. Don't put on tennis shoes! It just looks like an atrocity. There are the casual dress shoes that folks can get away with that aren't tennis shoes, but they aren't actual dress shoes either. Just make sure your shoes match and that the dress socks you have on aren't super distracting. Please have on DRESS socks, not white Nike socks. Again - tacky. Darker colors for your socks are appropriate, or if they are a light color, they should once again match the tone of your suit.

Hair:

As Black professionals, we get scrutinized much more than our white counterparts. As a recruiter, they will already judge you based on appearances, like a book by its cover, and that is just amplified for a Black person because that's how the world has been trained to view us anyway. We are seen as threatening even from a young age, especially for our young Black boys. Young Black girls are perceived as promiscuous and more developed/womanish than white girls, so they are treated as such - stripping away their innocence.

It isn't fair, nor is it right. It's something we navigate daily and people are fighting hard to change it. So, of course, when it comes to the battle of "hair," we know the narrative isn't different. We often hear stories on the news of Black people being fired or discriminated against because of how our hair NATURALLY grows out of our heads or the styles we decide to wear for protection, culture, etc. How many Black men do you know that shaved their dreads and spoke about how they were treated "more positively" after the fact? We know white people aren't looked at as sharply when it comes to their hair. They might get told to dye it back to a "natural" color, if anything.

So, what is my advice and view on this? I have heard other Black women give advice on work calls to not show up to an interview in braids. "Once you get in, *then* you can show your real self."

Now, I understand that point of view and even had it at one point and time. If this is how you feel, that is your prerogative. I'm just at the point now where I feel that if you don't want to hire me or do business with me because of my hair - then *YOU. AREN'T. FOR. ME. ANYWAY.* This has been the norm for so long, and we act like it's actually healthy and normal, but it's *not.* That is still discrimination. That is still racist. That is still toxic behavior.

We struggle enough to keep our coils from frizzing up and holding in a style as it is. Or to look clean-shaven and keep those waves on deck. You want me to change the tone of who I am to make *you* more comfortable when you say blatantly disrespectful stuff daily in the workplace and think it's fine? When all of you out here being micro-aggressive or just bold as hell in your statements or trying to touch *on* my hair? Hell to the nah, nah, nah!

Granted, I had more freedom as a business owner, but even going back into a corporate setting, I still will be my authentic self. The great thing about interviewing with a Black owned startup is that both me and my interviewer had braids! And that was a talking point for us as well. With that being said, that is a decision that you will have to make for yourself in the confines of a corporate setting. I won't be the one to shame you or make you feel bad either way. It's a free country, and it's your life. But I will just challenge you to think about it this way - if you have to compromise yourself to get hired/get your foot in the door, in what other ways will they make you compromise once you're actually in it for real? Just don't walk into an interview looking like you just rolled out of the bed. Your hair *should* be done, even if it's slicked up into a nice bun. Businesses always want to tout inclusivity. But they have gotten so "inclusive" to the point that it's truly exclusive. But that's a conversation for a different day.

At the end of the day, you want to feel confident in whatever it is that you're wearing because if you look great, then you'll feel great (including your hair). You're more than likely to have a better interview. You'll definitely be feeling yourself, not in a cocky way, but in the "I can do this, and I bring so much to the table" way.

Technology:

If you happen to be on a virtual call, be sure ahead of time to check your tech. It would be so unfortunate if your laptop died in the middle of your call or your internet went out because your little brother/sister, your husband/wife, or someone in the house was playing their video games online and sucked up all broadband. Have your computer charged ahead of time or keep it plugged in while you are interviewing. Also log into the software about 10 minutes ahead of time to make sure that your microphone and camera are connected, that the software loads properly, or that you can fix any issues before the actual interview is supposed to start. I normally have to start my Zoom application at least 5 minutes before I plan to use it because it takes forever to load on my desktop.

Environment:

Make sure that you are in a quiet space; you don't want a bunch of loud noise interrupting your conversation.

I know we've all seen the commercials of people locking themselves in bathrooms and trying to escape from their kids and whoever else may be at home. Luckily, people are more understanding now because this has been going on for over two years, so just make the best of the situation if you can and have someone else monitor your family as you are on your calls if possible.

Another thing to do is ensure your background is clear of clutter. Virtual backgrounds exist for a reason, but make sure it is appropriate for the setting. You don't want your favorite TV character sitting in the background while you're trying to interview, distracting everybody. Our department had a running joke with DJ Khaled as our background because HR would have to issue out all the policies for COVID and do the contact tracing. And every hour or even every minute, it felt like we just kept getting another case, so we had DJ Khaled with the caption "and another one" as the background for everyone who was in our department. That was more of a conversation starter and also helped us to emphasize that people need to make sure they're taking the precautions to be safe in their workstations and spaces. However, we were already established in the company, and it was agreed upon within our department, so don't do this during your interviews. Have a blurred background or a clean space in your home or one of the virtual backgrounds that look like an office or something of that nature.

I also want to run through some things not to do.

Basic don'ts:

Do not argue with people during your interview. If you have a difference of opinion, you can respectfully acknowledge their points and disagree by giving your take or your experience or research. But do not argue with folks; it will leave a bad taste in everyone's mouth. And it will make it seem like you can't control your emotions and are not level-headed.

No one wants to work with someone who they feel may be volatile. What happens if a deal comes up and you lose your cool and cost the company millions of dollars? So keep your composure even if you are flustered or taken off guard; remember to approach the situation with respect, acknowledge their point, give your angle, and keep it pushing. You can also read the situation to see if it's even worth giving a remark. Sometimes whoever you're talking to may be bullheaded, and it's better to just let things rock. You can thank them for whatever it is they advised and you'll consider it moving forward, whatever.

This isn't likely to happen as they will ask questions to get to know you better and see how your experience can fit within the role, but I've seen it happen. As Black people, we are already pegged as being "angry" or "aggressive" anyway. That will just give them another reason to misrepresent your character.

You also don't want to be cocky. A lot of times, *cockiness is a cover-up for incompetence.* A lot of times, when folks start to dig deeper, the person who's being cocky may not have an answer at the end of it, and they end up looking foolish. So don't come in as a know-it-all. Don't come in as someone who isn't coachable. Don't come in as someone who is an expert in everything in life. That is the ultimate turn-off.

You are working on building rapport and a relationship with these people and marketing your value. Therefore, if you're coming in hot, it may not bode well for you. Folks will not want to work with you or invest in you. Now you can be confident. *There is a fine line between confidence and cockiness.* But the difference lies in your ability to seek counsel and be coached. You are clearly there for a reason, so obviously you do not know everything, and you need some guidance or want further development within a role or company. Thus, you can come to the plate with the awesome value you have to offer and also be humble in the fact that you are willing to grow and learn.

Another mistake that people tend to make is that they talk too much. And this can go in multiple ways. If you're being asked a question, and you just start going on tangents that diverge from what was asked, it makes you look incompetent and as if you don't listen. It also can start feeding into the cocky side, which is what you don't want, given what I just said above.

A coworker and I were virtually interviewing somebody for a new leader role. One of the candidates was so self-assured and cocky. She was talking to us as if she were a godsend. She had a lot of experience but just spoke as if she were going to come in and fix everything. And we could tell she wasn't listening to some of the questions we were asking because her responses conflicted with what we actually had going on.

She kept talking about herself as if she were the greatest thing since sliced bread and wouldn't let us get a word in edgewise. We wanted to ask some clarifying questions or correct her on some things that she was saying, but she was so caught up in her own story that it was like we weren't even there. So my coworker and I were literally texting each other back and forth about her in the middle of the interview. We zoned out and stopped listening, and we were just ready for the interview to be over, and we ended it earlier than it needed to be.

If she had approached us in a way that had let us know that she was qualified but also was willing to learn more about how *we* did things within our company and not necessarily how things were happening at *her* company as if they directly translated, we would have been more open to having her as a top candidate. She had a lot of experience that could have been helpful to a degree, but how she presented herself made no one who talked to her want to continue being involved. Again, the mistakes she made were: coming off as cocky, presenting herself as if she would not need any training or coaching once she arrived, being very self-centered, and not listening to the questions being asked.

And to emphasize, my coworker and I were talking about her via text *in the middle* of the interview. And that is something you do not want to happen when you are vying for a role. If it gets to the point where your interviewers are checked out and over you, you've lost your opportunity. And that is what we don't want to happen.

Another mistake (and another one) people make is that they tend to harp on their weaknesses. For instance, if you're being asked about areas of opportunity and growth. The main thing you're supposed to do is list an area you know you have an opportunity in and discuss how you have been working on it and twist the story into a positive one. A lot of people tend to stay on the negative.

Example:

I could say in an interview that time management was something that I struggled with, but I have started utilizing my planner and calendar to mark specific times throughout the day to focus on certain tasks; through that, I am learning to manage my time better and can accomplish more than I have previously with efficiency.

You don't want to say, "Oh, I know that I haven't been the best at keeping track of my time, and so I'm just really struggling right now because I don't know what to do. And I just can't seem to find a system that works for me, so I'm still figuring it out right now. I just don't know."

That comes off as you not being a problem solver; it comes off as you being complacent in your lack of management with your time, and it makes the interviewer feel like they won't be able to trust you in a role, especially where it's important to have time management or if you're managing a team.

You need to think about things from the perspective of your interviewer. Because if the answers you give are causing any type of doubt that is detrimental, then you will not be pursued any longer for whatever that position is. People want to feel secure that you are self-aware and that you are motivated, coachable, and always trying to learn and grow.

The last thing we've already touched on is not being ill-prepared. So I'll just give a short synopsis of ensuring you are doing your due diligence to research the necessary info required for the day. Again, you won't know everything that's going on, so it's important to ask questions during the interview as part of your research. We'll discuss questions in the next chapter.

The moral of the story is that you want to be prepared going into your interview. And the best way to do this is to learn which format you'll be utilizing, whether in-person or virtual. Make sure you're doing your research. Be yourself, and dress the part. LISTEN to the questions that are being asked, and answer them without going off on tangents. If you do the work upfront, it'll make it easier during and on the backend. Then you won't regret all the things you didn't do because you prepared diligently.

CHAPTER 12

The Mock Up

In this chapter, we are going to break down answering questions.

I want you to be confident in yourself, in your values and experiences, and to speak to them clearly and concisely. That way, there's no confusion, and folks know exactly what you bring to the table and why they'll need your services. Also, be sure to focus on what they are asking and answer the question in full, as some may be two-part questions.

In general your answers should be no more than 2-3 minutes long, and a great format to utilize when answering questions is the C.A.R. method. It stands for Context, Action, and Results.

Context 20%:

The context is 20% of your answer, and it gives background information to the situation at hand. It is prepping your interviewer to know what was going on when you did whatever change or made whatever impact.

Action 60%:

The action is exactly what it sounds like. It's the action you took to make whatever happen in the context you just laid out. So if they're asking a question about your leadership, you're building the context around the situation and then you're speaking on the actions you took that show your leadership capabilities.

Results 20%:

The result is the impact of the action that you took. And it is important because it lets people understand what value came from your actions. If you created a campaign, but then it lost the company $500,000, that leadership action wasn't a great one, and it makes people think that maybe they can't trust your judgment. Unless it's a question around a time that you learned something or something didn't go the way you thought it would. Then you would have to spin it into a positive just like we spoke about in the previous chapter, around taking a weakness and turning it into a strength or a learning point and how you've grown from that. The result should answer the question: "So what"?

So let's do an example to make it clearer:

You are asked to tell about a time you had to make a change within your department or company.

An example I would give is from my own experience when I was working in a nonprofit as follows:

Context: We work with Black and Latino students and put them into paid internships with Fortune 500 companies as well as work on their college access. We had a lot of students who wanted to go to HBCUs (Historically Black Colleges & Universities) but were discouraged by the program coordinators because they didn't understand their importance in the Black community or the historical significance if they weren't the top five known schools.

Action: As the only person on staff who went to an HBCU, someone who graduated from Spelman - the number ONE Historically Black College and University - and understands their importance, especially within the black community, I called a meeting with our office and asked my manager to put me at the end of our agenda to discuss the issues. When I had the floor, I laid out all of the reasoning behind why Historically Black Colleges and Universities are important, regardless of if they are in the top five or the top 100, and how a lot of them are just as great and sometimes even better than the community colleges and other schools that we were sending our students to within the area. And that they needed to respect those schools and do their research before discouraging our students just because they didn't understand. I also explained why it was damaging to our students and that the coordinators were doing them a disservice and not providing them with the help we promised.

Results 20%: From this meeting, the director and my manager thanked me for opening their eyes to a new perspective, and we ended up creating educational resources on

HBCUs that the program coordinators utilized when discussing schools with our students. They were better informed to help them figure out which schools would be good fits, and 25% more of our students ended up applying to those HBCUs and even getting in.

That was the gist of the situation of what happened. Still, you see how there was an issue that I outlined through the context, and then discussed the action that I took in order to address the issue, and then the results that happened because I took that initiative. It also answers the question of how I influenced the department or the company. The "so what" is that 25% more students applied to schools, the staff had a better understanding of HBCUs which translated to our students, and resources were created.

Keep in mind that you can't give every detail of what was going on, but you have to provide enough to paint a picture of why whatever you did was important and why the results were impactful. There was a lot more that went into that story that I didn't go into, but I had to be clear and concise enough for them to get the picture overall and see how what I did had an impact. This story is an example of what I used in my interviews, not necessarily word for word, but the premise is the same.

Even though I was fairly new to the organization at this point, I was valued as a team member and brought some knowledge to the table that the rest of the staff did not. This is where having experience and knowledge, and the ability to do something only how YOU can do it comes in handy. They were open and willing to listen to me because I also brought a solution. You always want to make sure that you are solution-oriented and not someone who just points out all the problems but has no ideas to fix them. Even if you don't know how to fix it, maybe you can draw other people to help bring about a solution.

That'll help us start getting into the questions that you will be faced with, and the first one I'll start with (one that we thoroughly covered toward the beginning of this book) is:

Tell me about yourself/Walk me through your resume:

As we discussed, it doesn't matter who you are or what you're doing. People will always want to know more about you when they initially meet you and get to know you. This makes sense because how else will they know how to go in your relationship?

So knowing this, when you are meeting with an interviewer, you'll be asked either to talk about yourself or do a resume walk through, in which case you'll go through your resume in chronological or reverse order, depending. You'll discuss your experiences, giving more detail than what's written on the bullets, give more detail about your skills and schooling, all that jazz.

Luckily, we already broke down how to answer this question earlier on, so by this point, you should be a pro at it if you've been practicing with friends and family or your mirror.

With that being said, we can move on to the rest. Generally there are three categories of interview questions: Behavioral, Situational, Case based questions.

There are six categories that Behavioral questions can fall into. Majority of interviewers pull from these same categories because those are the skills they want to see within whatever role it is. You have certain functionalities that will add in case questions like consulting or even marketing, so those are also things to be aware of and prepare for.

Now I'm not an expert in cases, so I won't go into full detail on that here, but I would suggest looking up different tools that companies utilize as they are doing cases. I will list a few examples of what case questions may look like, but I won't necessarily go through them.

The last type would be a situation-based question which is similar to a case but not 100%. You are literally role-playing what you would do in a situation with the interviewers, or in a less extreme version, walking them through what you would do. This happened to me at one of my interviews, and it completely caught me off guard because no one spoke about it before the career fair I went to. So I will touch on that as well.

Behavioral Questions:

General questions that you are most likely guaranteed to get asked outside of the tell me about yourself would be:

- What are your greatest strengths/weaknesses?

You should have this one in the bag because you've spent all that time reflecting on those strengths and accomplishments. You have also reflected on your weaknesses and know not to harp on them. List one and what you have been doing to learn or grow from it and pivot into the results from such.

- What is the toughest problem you faced? What did you do to solve it? What would you do differently? (or some variation of this)

This question will look at your ability to analyze and problem solve. It will also dictate whether you are good under pressure or not. You can say that you wouldn't necessarily do anything differently because it was a learning experience for you, and you will utilize that knowledge moving forward when similar situations arise. Or you could say that knowing what you know now, you would have approached it in xyz fashion to avoid xyz issues.

That can be seen as a tricky question. But feel free to answer it in what way feels best. Just make sure to say what you learned even if you would go back and do something differently.

- Why do you want to work for our firm/have this role (or) Why should we hire you? (some variation of this or what sets you apart from other candidates)

This is probably one of the more critical questions that people fumble on because they haven't done their due diligence to research the company enough to give a specific answer. This is why I said to ensure you are in tune with what the company has going on. They want to make sure you aren't just applying for the heck of it and will be an asset and you are dedicated to them.

Other questions that you may get will be around why that specific industry, how would you describe yourself, or how would a close friend, colleague, or parent describe you? If you are in school for a graduate program, you may be asked why you chose that specific school or why you're studying in your field, or you can be asked why you're career switching.

You also may be asked why you left/are leaving your previous role or job or something of that nature. These are just a few more questions that are pretty general to get asked. So make sure that you are doing your homework and looking up what's going on in your specific industry and with your specific company and how they compare to their competitors because those types of questions may also come up.

I am giving you a business school level game because even if you didn't go to business school or attend a graduate program, you need to approach these people in the same manner so that you stand out as a high-caliber candidate.

You may be going up against folks who did graduate from these programs, and you may have more experience and be more qualified than many of them. So, you need to be able to speak like them even if you aren't in those programs. That is the level of preparation that interviewers will be looking for. That is the level of polish they want from their candidates.

Onto the six categorical questions that interviewers use:

- Leadership
- Adaptability
- Culture Add
- Collaboration

- Growth Potential
- Prioritization

If you sat in an interview, all of these should sound familiar. They can show up in different forms, but these categories are touched on at least once during the line of questioning.

Your interviews will take anywhere from 30 minutes to an hour, depending on where you are in the stage of recruitment and if you're on a panel or with a singular interviewer. The last ten or so minutes will be utilized for you to ask any questions to get clarity on anything, and to review the next steps.

I want you to think of your interview as a time to showcase your skills and learn more about the company to see if you really want to work there. I said earlier that it is a two-way street. It's not just if you're a fit for them, but also if they are a fit for you. As long as you remember this, you don't need to go into the interview nervous.

If you have prepped ahead of time, are confident in your experiences, and have at least two to three examples per question type, you should be fine. Just be yourself, have fun, and learn what you can while you can. You are gaining access to the person who may be your manager or someone on that team or department. Figure out as much as you can from them on topics that you can't really research online. That way, when the offer comes, you can make an informed decision and feel confident in your choice.

I realize that you can't prepare a hundred percent for everything they'll ask you. There's always at least one question that will throw you off guard to some degree. When that happens, just take a moment to collect your thoughts, don't feel pressured or rushed, and answer the question like you've done for the others you prepared for.

Just know that you have a story logged away in your mind that will answer the question asked; you just have to relax enough to draw it out. I know you've probably had an experience where after the fact, you were like, "Oh, I could have used this answer for that question! I'm so stupid!" because I've definitely had a moment or two like that. So let's get into the questions.

Leadership:

Leadership questions will always be in the mix because they don't plan on you staying at an entry-level or managerial level forever. They want to know that you are somebody who can grow in the company and develop the people under you or handle and lead projects that will bring the company success. 50% of people leave the company not necessarily because of the job but because they've had terrible leaders and bosses. So this is a great time to think back on any clubs back in school that you held a leadership position in, if you were the president or founder of an organization or company, if you were the committee chair on an advisory board or within an organization, or whatever projects that you've led currently at your job or in the past.

These are all the areas you need to reflect on and have at the ready when you're asked these questions. Some questions can double as well, and it might not necessarily be you leading a group of people. It can also be how you led through change or some type of crisis, conflict management, or within a team setting. It can also be around how you influenced key stakeholders or your supervisor. Those things all still apply to being a leader.

1. Tell me about the toughest decision you had to make in the last six months.

This question is looking for your ability to not only seek help when needed but also the ability to make an executive decision. Many of us may describe ourselves as being indecisive, which can be detrimental as a leader. This is something that I've had to learn because I am very good at creating and founding new things and getting people on board to follow me, but I am also very concerned about everyone else's well-being.

You can't please everyone, and at the end of the day, you are the leader and need to make the decision. They look up to you to do so. Ben Horowitz speaks about it a lot in his book "The Hard Thing about Hard Things" as well, which helps bring a lot of insight to this topic. So now, I am less hesitant to just make a decision for the group even if it ends up being the "wrong" one. At least you made a decision within an appropriate amount of time. Because they also don't want to see that you let things fester if they should be nipped in the bud.

2. Tell me about the last time something significant didn't go according to plan at work. What was your role and/or the outcome?

This question is really just looking to see how you take accountability within the scope of your work. It's another reflection point for yourself to see what you learned from the experience and if you would have done anything differently. Remember that answering interview questions should focus on you. You don't want to shift blame to other people or talk badly about other folks within your answers.

3. Describe a situation where you needed to persuade someone to see things your way. What steps did you take? What were the results?

This question will be looking for credibility and how you utilize your resources or evidence to influence. It's not necessarily that you know best or that you know everything, but taking what you do know and your personal relationships or influence to navigate other people within your organization.

4. Describe your leadership style - when does it work/when doesn't it? (or what type of leader are you? variation)

You're guaranteed to get this question, especially depending on the type of role you're applying to. At least as an MBA candidate, this question definitely came up a lot in my interviews. Knowing your leadership style will help you, and knowing the types of styles that you don't want to be will help you craft an answer for this as well.

If you had a manager who was micromanaging you, who wasn't very helpful or resourceful, or any other unattractive quality, then you know that these are not characteristics that you want as a leader. Name things like servant-leadership or leading by example; a transparent leader, an adaptable leader, or whatever fits your actual style.

There are a plethora of leadership questions that we can go through, but these are pretty good ones that you'll either get asked or some variation of the question may be asked. During all of my interviews, I've had some variation of one of these questions. To keep prepping, you can look up different leadership questions online. I would just make sure to pay attention to the source it's coming from and its credibility. The questions I'm listing out will be a mix of ones I've experienced, some from business school interview prep, and similar questions to different HR guides. LinkedIn is also a great source as well.

Adaptability:

This skillset is highly important, especially in a rapidly changing industry or fast-paced work environment. 69% of hiring managers are said to look for this skill within their potential new employees. As technology changes and things in the world change, having people on the team who aren't set in their ways and can navigate new conditions and environments will be beneficial to the company or department.

Knowing when to adapt is also important, but is something that can be debated until the end of time. If you need some inspiration around adaptability, reading the book "Who Moved My Cheese" will give you an insight on people stuck in their ways versus folks who rush in versus those who adapt over time.

1. Describe a situation in which you embraced a new system, process, technology, or idea at work that was a major departure from the old way of doing things.

The interviewer will be looking to see if you embraced the new change, if you're eager to learn and move forward within the change, and even if you found a better way to improve things.

2. Describe an example or two of a situation that required you to take quick action. What criteria did you use in making your decisions?

This question looks to see how well you analyze a situation in a confined space of time and under pressure. They want to know how you think through the process and why you came up with the solution you did. Are you quick to react, or do you allow yourself to procrastinate before taking action?

3. Recall a time when you were assigned a task outside your job description. How did you handle the situation? What was the outcome?

This question here just gave me all types of traumatic flashbacks. As someone who worked in nonprofit or even within HR, you are wearing multiple hats at almost all times. And it can get to the point where the work you're supposed to be doing isn't getting done because you're being stretched thin in every other direction.

Have an answer for this question, and know that it may come and don't get triggered by it in the moment. You can be a human, of course. I've had my times where I sighed or scoffed, saying, "Oh, there's so many situations, where do I begin?" and laughed to bring it back and not make it seem so negative.

Again even if it was a negative experience, you don't want it to come off as just being completely terrible and switch the mood of the interview. They are looking to see if you're willing to learn something new because eventually, as you get promoted, you will be going beyond your current capabilities and taking on new things that were outside of your initial role description. You may also start getting asked to do things outside of your role that may be building up to that promotion. So, folks are gauging whether you're a complainer or will take a chance to do something new and find ways to succeed in that new environment.

Culture Add:

This is more on the new school of thought of how managers approach candidates. Previously, it was more so are you a "culture fit" versus "culture add"? The difference is that a culture fit will just uphold your current culture, whereas a culture add will enhance it and help it grow over time. Just like with the last section of adaptability, cultures may shift within a company at any given moment in time, and if you're someone who adds to that shift versus just trying to stick to the old ways, things will fare much better for you and the company as a whole. This is important for when companies get acquired, and they may be looking to downsize a department and re-interview all of the employees. It can help you to stand apart.

Culture adds can also help the company shift into a more positive environment than where it may be currently. There's nothing wrong with being a culture fit in and of itself, but you also want to *add* to the company's dynamic. They just don't want a bunch of people who are all the same anymore and don't bring about new ideas or improvements to the culture.

They're also looking for folks who align with the company's values, mission, and vision. With everything that went down with George Floyd's murder and all of the companies (especially the ones in Minneapolis) taking a stance around Black Lives Matter, we could see as a nation the different cultural shifts that were happening within the companies themselves. They shift toward recognizing and *seeing* Black people and the traumas we carry to work with us daily. Providing safe spaces to speak about and educate our white counterparts and have them take more initiative as well as "allies." So, of course, Black people everywhere within these companies started to step up around some of these shifts that were happening and helped to curate some of those shifts as well.

This is also why I emphasized for you as the candidate to ask the questions that are tough and will make them reveal any of those shifts that they may have had within their culture to see if they are a fit/add for you too. Many companies had lip service until that tragedy happened, and then they had to put their money where their mouth was... literally. So these are the types of things that you also need to consider for your personal sanity and mental health when going to work for these companies.

1. What's the biggest misconception your coworkers have about you, and why do they think that?

This question looks to see how self-reflective, self-aware, and transparent you are. They will also be looking to see how well you communicate or how open you are with the people within your work. I will add that this doesn't mean you need to tell everyone your business, as we know that many of our white counterparts overshare about their personal lives and make things a bit uncomfortable. This is more so around just being open and willing to have conversations with people on a decent level, not necessarily about your drunken weekends or any drama that's taking place in your life.

2. Tell me about a time in the last week when you've been satisfied, energized, and productive at work. What were you doing?

This question is to gauge that your environment and the type of work you're doing is right for you, or to hear how that type of work is good for you on their end.

3. What would make you choose our company over others?

This is another transparency type of question where you will give more of an honest answer and not necessarily something that you think the company wants to hear. It also can help them see the type of competitor analysis happening and any perks they may have over similar companies.

Collaboration:

More likely than not, you'll be working in some type of team setting. When you have a group of people who can work well together, they are more productive, and the work environment itself is healthier. So managers don't want to introduce someone into the mix who may be cancerous within a healthy environment, bringing down productivity and creating a toxic atmosphere for the other employees. Working well with others isn't just something from your childhood; it plays a part in all areas of life.

1. Give an example of when you had to work with someone who was difficult to get along with. How did you handle interactions with that person?

This question may be difficult for some people because you may want to go on the defensive or throw your partner under the bus. Refrain from doing this because it will only make you look bad and as if you are the difficult person. For all my Libras out there who are well-balanced, this is a question searching to see how well you can see issues from another person's perspective in addition to your own. Seeing both sides of the story is important when making decisions so that you aren't just acting selfishly but can weigh the pros and cons and come up with a fair solution that is most likely centered on facts versus opinions.

2. Can you share an experience where a project dramatically shifted direction at the last minute? What did you do?

When I was asked this question in an interview early on in my career, I loosely came up with an answer for it that luckily satisfied my interviewer. Still, they did dig deeper, and I had to finesse the situation at hand to answer the follow-ups. You don't want to have to finesse, so be prepared. Now I have loads of examples where I wouldn't need to finesse, so think of the different situations you've been in where this applies.

Here, interviewers are looking to see how well you can keep the team on track and seek help or even direction from your team as needed in an unexpected situation. The good thing about this question is that there is usually always some answer you can give because things are always ever-changing within the work environment. So just make sure that you have your answer well-crafted in case they decide to ask a few follow-up questions.

3. Explain what you have done to build trust among team members?

This is a great question for those in business school or any other type of graduate programs because you are most likely in a cohort and have a core team with which you work on most projects. The Kelley School of Business thrives on collaboration and teamwork, which set it apart in many ways from other schools, especially when we were going into our internships and full-time offers. That was a lot of the feedback that our graduate career services received from Fortune 500 Companies. Since everyone may have different working styles, it is good to build rapport on your team and trust that folks will help you to better finish your projects. So knowing how you establish trust on your team is a great way for managers to gauge how you will work with other people and have considerations for their strengths and weaknesses as well as your own. In addition, make sure to have follow through on your part of the projects, understand how to utilize everyone on your team's strengths and know people's weaknesses within the scope of your projects.

Growth Potential:

Are you here just applying because you really need a job or to develop within the company? Companies don't want to hire you just to have you leave within the next year or so. it takes one and a half to two times an employee's salary to replace them. It is more expensive for a company to lose you than to keep you, so it's in their best interest to hire people that they can see will grow within the company or at least have the potential to. Even if you do just need a job and don't plan to stay at the company long, you'll need to portray that you are planning around longevity to at least get your foot in the door.

They will also be looking for people who can grow into the role and may not necessarily have exactly everything it takes to go right into it, depending on the situation and the need. They also know that you will want to grow within a company and won't want to be doing the same thing because that can lead to boredom and eventually bring about attrition.

1. Describe a time when you volunteered to expand your knowledge at work instead of being directed to do so.

This shows that you were actively willing to learn and continue to seek out new opportunities for your own development. Employers also want to know that you are eager and will seek out resources as needed.

2. Recall a time when your manager was unavailable when a problem arose. How did you handle the situation? Who did you consult with?

This situation shows that you know how to step up to the plate with some leadership capabilities. It also shows how you assess situations and the different stakeholders you may need to involve without stepping on anyone's toes or going over people's heads.

Prioritization:

All these will show your ability to effectively manage your time, meet deadlines or tight schedules, and have great attention to detail. This is the top third quality that managers desire for their candidates to have. Organization not only helps you but will keep whatever projects you are handling running smoothly, which in turn helps the company run more smoothly.

1. Tell me about a time when you had to juggle several projects simultaneously. How did you organize your time? What was the result?

The interviewer will be looking to see what processes or systems you put in place to keep track of your projects and how you decided to rank them and complete them. Do you seek the advice of management in these decisions or other key stake-holders? How are you spending your time, how does your calendar look, and how do you ensure you meet deadlines?

2. Give an example of a time when you delegated an important task successfully.

Here you understand what you can and cannot handle on your plate and therefore are detailed and organized in handing off tasks to others. They will look to see how you set deadlines and expectations for others.

Extra Function Specific Questions:

Because everyone may be going into different industries or functionalities, I will list two questions from the main functions that people go into so you can have an idea of the questions that may arise for those roles and not just the general ones. Keep in mind you may be asked different questions. These are ones that just seem to be more detailed in the functionality. Even if you aren't asked these specific ones, they can be helpful to still think through as you prep.

Corporate Finance/Strategy:

1. How would you go about valuing our "division" for a potential sale, spin-off, or liquidation?

2. Our (blank) division is thinking about introducing a new widget product. How would you go about determining if this is a good idea or not?

Consulting:

Again within Consulting, you will most likely have some type of case interview. Case interviews assess candidates and their analytical skills in a pressured, real-time environment. The questions are usually business problems, arithmetic, logic problems, or estimating exercises to make you think on your toes, use common sense, or reason.

The point of case interviews is not to get them right, because there most often isn't a right answer, but instead is designed to analyze your ability to solve complex problems and see how you think. You can bounce ideas off of your interviewer, ask questions to seek clarification, etc. This is encouraged since you will be working in a team environment during your actual job. You will use pen and paper to take notes and perform any calculations needed to come up with your answer.

Case Question Types:

This is not an exhaustive list but some of the more common types of questioning. Please seek case consulting materials to help you prep ahead of time.

- Market sizing - could be asked to estimate the size of a particular product; use a mix of assumptions and estimates to justify your logic.
- Pricing - increasing revenue or pricing forms are normal for this type, and the interviewer will look to see which approach you choose.
- Go/No-go Market Entry Decision - focus on multiple aspects like barriers to entry, future growth, core capabilities, industry, competition, etc.

- M&A (Mergers & Acquisitions) - this is popular since many companies face these scenarios a lot in real life. Management capabilities, synergies, profitability/growth, etc., are all things tested.
- NPV/Breakeven - you test a project's viability by analyzing either NPV or breakeven point.

General Consulting Questions:

1. Why Consulting? Why this firm?
2. Give me an example of a business problem and tell me how you solved it?

Health Care Management:

3. What are the attributes of management success in the healthcare industry?
4. What are the most important issues emerging in healthcare currently? Prioritize them.
5. Choose one of these issues and give some recommendations on addressing it:
   a. Managed care
   b. HCA fallout
   c. Any other current or controversial issue in healthcare

Human Resources (my jam!)

As a previous HR professional, I will say that one thing you do not want to do during this interview is to say that you want to help people, and that's why you are going into HR. There are a plethora of other industries and functionalities you can move in to help people. Nobody wants to hear that generic answer from you, or you will be thrown out of the candidate pool.

Your answer needs to be something specific and concrete. The reason I gave was that I was interested in professionally developing others and bringing the importance of human capital to the forefront within these companies because it is missing a lot of times.

1. Describe a change effort you have undertaken. What was your role? What specifically did you do?
2. Tell me about a time you identified a gap in your organization's culture/infrastructure and how you chose to address/fix it?
3. What is your approach to client management, and how do you build relationships?
4. What are your three immediate priorities if you get this role?

Other questions will vary based on if you are going into recruiting, employee relations, generalist, compensation & benefits, payroll, systems management (like Workday), and other factors. Many questions will deal with influencing business strategy even if you don't have a leadership position, influencing stakeholders, training/onboarding, etc.

IB - Investment Banking (general)

1. What stocks do you follow and why?
2. How would selling a long-term bond affect all three financial statements?
3. If a company has a consistent negative earning record and wanted to raise capital and could only do so by

issuing debt, what type of debt should they issue and why?

IB - sales and trading:

1. Sell me this pencil (yes - this sounds crazy, but I've heard people tell stories of how they had a question like this in their interviews!)
2. Describe an instance where you persuaded someone to do something they didn't initially want to do.
3. What does the yield curve look like? What does it mean?

Marketing - (general)

I just want to note that marketing spans multiple functionalities and isn't just the stuff you see on TV. For those with marketing backgrounds, you are well aware. But for those who don't, consumer insights, brand management, product management, etc., all play a role in marketing. You have your 5 Ps (people, product, placement, pricing, promotion), amongst other things. Then you have B2B (business to business) vs. B2C (business to consumer) marketing. The Kelley School of Business has two great programs for these areas if you are interested in an MBA program (and no, this is not sponsored).

1. What are the attributes of a successful marketing campaign?
2. Tell me about an advertising campaign that you find effective/ineffective?
3. Give an example of an innovative solution to a business problem.

Marketing - Brand Management (the good stuff)

This is another area where you may be hit with some case questions. They will have to do with market share and things of that nature. Look up extra resources online to find examples of some marketing cases.

1. Pick a product and position it.
2. How do you calculate market share?
3. Define market segmentation. Picket a brand and segment it for me.
4. Pretend today is your first day at our company as a brand manager over brand x. What are the ten most important questions you'd ask to find out about the brand?

MIS (Management Information Systems)

1. Have you implemented a change project? What problems have you faced?
2. In what ways have you utilized existing technologies?
3. Have you dealt with client/server networks before? Token Rings? Intranet programs like Notes or Exchange?

Venture Capital:

1. In addition to high tech ventures, where do you think VC money should be going?
2. Have you had to deal with failure in a professional context?
3. What do you look for in a venture? Which is more important, the product or the people behind it?

4. Do you think emphasis should be put on raising money and putting it to work or on the human capital?

Random questions to catch you off-guard:

1. Is it better to submit a project that's perfect and late, or good and on time?
2. It's 12 pm a year from now. What are you doing?
3. Why shouldn't I hire you?

These are just examples again of different questions you may be asked for these specific industries. Look up other questions that are most widely asked and speak to people in these functions that you know who can help you prepare for the interview or to learn the different skills and capabilities needed to enter these industries.

Another tip to help you prep for all of these functions and positions is utilize the job descriptions and key role responsibilities to also come up with the types of questions you may be asked. For example, if you are trying to become a recruiter and the day to day involves you sourcing candidates, you'll most likely be asked a question around how you previously sourced candidates, the systems you used, how you filled the pipeline, etc. So use the role descriptions to your advantage and match what your responsibilities would be to any experiences that you've had in your previous roles.

Situational Based Questions:

I mentioned before that I had a situation case question pop up in one of my interviews, and it threw me off guard. This was for an automotive company I dearly wanted to work for (and I got the offer but decided to go elsewhere). So, I was sitting with two interviewers, and after we finished discussing a plethora of questions, they handed me a packet. One of them explained that we were going to role-play a situation they see all the time in their plants due to them having a union and whatnot. They were going to give me five minutes to look over the information, and then when they came back, we would get into character.

Now, only *one* of them was role-playing (which they didn't make clear until after we started), and the other was just watching. Thankfully, I have some tough skin and had dealt with some unruly folks before because the interviewer all but cussed me out over the situation at hand. Basically, there was a grievance filed, and I was over the case and couldn't do anything until legal came back with some instructions, but the union rep wasn't having that and was trying to argue me down (in my "office") about it.

So I handled my business, even though I was nervous as heck, but decided to find the fun in it since I love to act and looked at it as a practice/learning situation.

Afterward, they asked me how I felt I did. I don't remember what I said, but it was something to the effect of I think I did well for not experiencing that environment before but knew there were probably a few things I could've handled better. Then I asked them what *they* thought since that was the more important question. They just looked at each other, then looked back at me not saying anything. At that moment, I was like, dang - I didn't think I bombed it *that* bad. They must've seen the look on my face and were like, "We're going to offer you the position!" So, there you go, lol.

The second "scenario" based situation was more of the CPG company presenting me with a hypothetical situation and then asking what I would do if I were the manager or something or other.

They gave me a moment to think about it, and then I answered, and they loved what I said. That was also a great interview because I connected with one of them based on the nonprofit I had worked at beforehand. The company she had worked for previously partnered with them, so we talked for a good ten minutes about that experience (diverting from the interview and allowing the interviewer to reminisce and talk about themselves, which is always great), then returned to it.

So - just a reminder to make sure you BUILD RAPPORT in your interviews. You never know what random points you'll connect on. But anyway, those are some scenario-based examples you may run into.

Questions for YOU to ask them

I've said it once, and I'll repeat it. When you are sitting in the interview for a role, you need to ask questions. This is the way for you to find out what issues there may be ahead of time, if this person or company is a fit or add to you, and to get some details that you may not be able to find elsewhere.

Rule of Thumb:

Have at LEAST three to five questions ready for them before you get to the interview. I say at least three to five because as you are speaking, they may answer some of them for you in passing. While speaking to them, they may say something you want to know more about - so you write it down as a question for the end.

Your questions can fall across a span of categories:

- Team/department expectations
- What your first 90 days will look like or the type of support/training they have in place for your role
- DEI (diversity, equity & inclusion)/social corporate responsibility, company culture, things of that nature
- How the employees are evaluated and how often
- Do they have a work-life balance, or what's the company's view on such?
- Personal questions that you found about your interviewer on LinkedIn pertaining to their career path/future
- Things they like or dislike about the company/projects/department
- Challenges or key opportunities for the role you're applying for

- Top 3 skills to be successful in that role
- How they feel about what they do playing a bigger part in the company, etc.
- So much more

At the end of the day, Make sure you are asking questions that are important to you that check off the boxes on your values list, work-life balance, company culture, what is expected of you and how your performance will be evaluated, team dynamics so you know what you're walking into, etc.

Also, make sure that you are clear on the next steps of the process so that you aren't waiting in limbo. Sometimes recruiters have a bad habit of ghosting candidates, which isn't fair to you. So if they say they will follow up within a week and you don't hear from them, feel free to send an email a couple of days after the week is up to check in (sometimes they get backlogged).

You want to be as sure and comfortable as possible when you decide to take that offer.

After the interview:

Make sure to send a thank you email or note to your interviewer within 24 hours of your interview. Now, I say 24 hours because you want to leave that immediate impression. They could have more interviews over a few days, and you might get lost in the chaos. Make sure to mention something from the interview you both related to or a story they told you to jog their memory. They interview loads of people. This is another way to help you stand out. Also reiterate a strength of yours that can contribute to the role/org and how you're excited about something the company is doing based on your discussion. You want to keep it short, meaningful, and again remind them of something great about yourself.

It doesn't need to be anything wild or crazy.

Just a subject line of:

Thank You for Your Time - Your Name.

You can then say you just wanted to reach out to thank them for taking the time to interview you. You enjoyed your conversation with them about xyz and wish them well with the rest of the process. You really are excited about the opportunity to utilize your (blank) skills within xyz manner. Look forward to hearing from them, Best Regards/Sincerely/etc. Your Name.

Most people don't do this, so again, it's a nice way to set yourself apart. Even if you had a bad interview, I'd still suggest it.

Also, the interview isn't over until you hang up the call (make sure you have completely exited the platform!) or until you are down the street from the office if it was in person.

Folks keep tabs on how you interact with people in the building, and you never know who knows who - so be nice to EVERYONE - especially the receptionist. Depending on how you treat them, they can make or break your chances.

After I was hired at my second nonprofit, they always joked about how I was super nice to the receptionist and felt bad that I let her give me some of her essential oils before the interview (so you never know what's going on).

Take notes, as I said before; you may get some good information you didn't know before and have questions based on what you learn. This can be pen and paper or on your laptop if you're virtual in OneNote or Word.

Be humble! Don't act like a know-it-all or a cocky clown; be yourself and have fun while still holding onto that professional element.

I got three offers in one day because I knew how to work the room with my interviewers. I'm personable, and people tend to have a great time in our interviews. We all usually ended on a high note with huge smiles and them stating they couldn't wait to show and tell me more.

The same was true for when I interviewed as a coach for this startup in Cali and my recent position with this Black owned startup.

Remember the interview where my classmate came up to me and said she'd never made her interviewers laugh or have a good time. She could hear us from outside of the booth we were in, and it made her nervous (and yes, I did get that offer). So make sure you go in confident, be relaxed, and take some breaths. Folks always love a good anecdote when it fits into the conversation. It all works together. If you are human and are engaging, it will be okay.

CHAPTER 13

Bonus Chapter: Extra Tips For Success

We've discussed all the different ways you can succeed during the recruiting process, but what about once you get the offer? Or what about even while you're working? I'll just leave a few tips here to help you thrive.

To start - once you get your offer letter and any other employment agreements - READ IT. Read the full document. People have a habit of just signing things without even looking at what they are signing. Look at the non-compete clauses, the compensation and benefits package, and any other requirements and clauses they have. Make sure you are in agreement, or add it to the list of things you'll want to negotiate. It can also help you decide if you want to decline the offer.

Negotiations:

Don't just accept the first thing they throw at you. There are levels to this.

1. Salary

There are many things that you can negotiate when it comes to your offer. 70% of employers expect people to negotiate. Obviously, we all know about salary. And you'll most likely have a verbal agreement of salary and other things before you get your written one. Let them tell you first before you put a number out there. If they ask what you expect for salary, let them know that you will need to have all of the information about benefits and other things before you can say what you feel a fair salary is. Or if it doesn't come up, ask them what the intended salary range is. They can then give you a number, and you negotiate. When you're filling out the job app, you can leave it blank or put zero if they require you to fill out the expected salary.

It's good to have an idea of the market range that people make for your type of role, and obviously, you know your value and experience and what you can bring to the table. Don't lowball yourself or let the company lowball you. Don't get too greedy, either. If you have other offers, you can also use this to your advantage.

I literally just negotiated $10,000 more onto my salary than the original range they were giving. The only person you are hurting is yourself when you don't ask. Factor in some of the other benefits as well and the industry you are in and the type of organization you are trying to work for. This can determine pay rate.

Many times as Black employees we are overworked and underpaid. There is always some type of wiggle room. Getting more on your salary from jump will put you lightyears ahead when it comes time for bonuses and promotions.

2. Signing Bonus

Negotiate how much you get as a signing bonus if they offer it upfront. If they don't offer a signing bonus, negotiate it into your offer - reasoning such as this will guarantee your employment for x amount of time (most companies usually have a 1 - 3 year minimum if you get a bonus to be employed). If you break your contract early, you'll normally have to pay back the bonus, so be cognizant of that. I had a signing bonus for my last company, and it was a one-year obligation. I left after a year and a few months (as did most people in my position who worked in the plants versus headquarters). Try to stick to factual information about your experience and things you can do to progress the company for your signing bonus. Experts recommend not adding much about your personal lifestyle into it. However, with inflation and everything, it's common sense to say that it'll help you settle down with the cost of living and rent prices skyrocketing. Use your best judgment.

Also make sure that you ask for it to be grossed up. This means that they are paying all of the taxes and you will get the full stated amount. The last thing you want is a $10k signing bonus, but then you really only get $6k-$7k after taxes.

3. Bonus/Commissions

Negotiate how often bonuses happen, the percentage, what goes into the bonus requirements, etc.

4. Remote/Hybrid

Depending on your function, most companies allow employees to work remotely (especially with COVID changing how we work). Some positions will be hybrid. You can negotiate how many days you go into the office a week or a month. Employers understand that work-life balance is very important to employees as folks have been more vocal since the pandemic.

5. PTO (paid time off)

You can negotiate how many days you get off a year, sick days, etc.

6. Relocation

Do they provide relocation? If not, ask for it. This can kind of mesh with a signing bonus. However, I received relocation and a signing bonus. If you don't need to relocate, see if this money can be repurposed for a signing bonus or other needs. Again, make sure to ask for it to be grossed up so you can get the full amount.

7. Flexible Work Schedule

Again, this can fall into the bucket with hybrid/remote work. You can make it known that you can't work past x time on specific days if you have kids and what have you. Or maybe you negotiate to work 4 days a week if you are staying on top of everything. You can request a trial period, etc.

8. Phone/Laptops/Home Office Set Up

This is especially important if you have a remote position. Having a work phone, work laptop, and budget to set up for a home office can be important if they expect you to comfortably work and have the resources you need.

9. Position/Job Title

If your title is a bit basic sounding, or the work correlates to a different title that might bode better for promotion time, or if you are job searching later on, this can be helpful. Program Coordinator versus Assistant Program Manager sound and look different on a resume or when someone is viewing your profile on LI (LinkedIn).

13. Other Items

You can also negotiate equity if it's a privately held company or startup. Other things you can negotiate involve Stock Options, Tuition Reimbursement if you would like to get your master's or go back to school, or get a certification that can help you advance in your career and will be positive for the company. They usually want to invest in things that will benefit them in the long haul, so they might require you to come back and work for x amount of years after receiving your degree. Make sure you negotiate this or are aware.

Another one that's in the same vein is professional training. Attending conferences, workshops, etc., that can help you grow in your career or current position can fall under training.

Make sure to do your research and speak with great negotiating folks or get some resources that can help you. One of my soRHOrs s specializes in negotiating and has a book, especially for women - Jacqueline Twillie. Look her up.

Managing Up

I touched on managing up earlier, but this is important regardless of where you are in your career. You can't be afraid to put your career in your own hands because, at the end of the day, no one cares about your progression like you do. No one truly has a vested interest like you. As you start your new position, you need to ensure that you and your manager are on the same page. That means laying out your goals and going through those development plans I mentioned earlier. It also means ensuring you are getting the onboarding and training you need. Most companies drop the ball when it comes to onboarding new employees and even when people are promoted into a new position.

Employees aren't clear on expectations. People get thrown into the fire with no real route for escape. If you need help, if you need clarity on project priorities, and if you need more guidance - let them know. Don't sit silently. Managers have their own things going on and aren't always in tune with their employees' needs. Don't pretend you are fine while drowning in the deep end. Set up meetings as frequently as needed to get comfortable. However, make sure that you are problem-solving on your own, and utilize your resources to do research, learn more about your projects, interfacing with different stakeholders, etc. Don't be 100% dependent on your manager but make sure they are meeting your needs and that you are showing and taking initiative on your own. No one likes to handhold folks. If you're new to your role, though, a little more hands-on approach is appropriate. Also, consult with coworkers and folks in similar positions if you aren't getting what you need from your manager.

Ask for projects or volunteer to help in areas that will give you an idea of the career path you believe you want to take. See if you can sit in on meetings to learn more about specific areas of your function or the company. I would sit in on meetings between operations and our technicians to learn about the projects they were working on, the budgets, the issues they were having on the floor, and how the machinery worked. It showed initiative and helped me have a well-rounded understanding of our business and ways I could help if needed. The technicians were shocked because, normally, HR wouldn't be in those meetings. Still, they were also appreciative because I took an actual interest in what they had going on and learned the terminology of what they were doing.

If you want a promotion, make sure you are letting your manager and other key power-players understand your goals. The same applies to taking action to get exposure to different types of projects, having coffee chats or shadowing people in areas you are looking to be promoted. Make sure your manager gives you tangible feedback on areas you can improve on that will set you up for success. Find out what skills or capabilities you need to grow. Find out the skills you already possess. Learn more about the interview process and how to speak to projects in a way that will set you apart from other candidates. Talk to people in those departments to get a better understanding of the day-to-day. Ask your manager to connect you with people. They are there to help you grow and progress - whether or not you do it there or at another company. If they don't do that, they aren't a great manager. You should have a clear picture of your career trajectory and the steps you can take to get there. If they don't do that, find someone in the company (mentor, champion, etc.) who will help you. If you can't get that at all, it's time to go elsewhere.

Rejection:

Throughout this process you may get some rejections, and that's perfectly normal. It doesn't mean you are a failure. I've definitely been turned down for a job or two, and those were normally ones I applied to cold turkey. Regardless, if they provide feedback or you're able to get feedback, utilize that as a learning experience for the next time. If the rejection comes after the interview, ask them for feedback so that you know how to mitigate any issues in your next interview.

Remember to continuously affirm yourself and know that you are more than capable. Lean on your connections and people in your network during this process. Most of these companies hire people based on employee referrals, which is why I implore you to network network network! Every job I've gotten (except my first one out of school and the career coaching one for the Cali startup) has been through a connection, including my most recent one with Combs Enterprises! So keep your head up and know that your time is coming.

Handle rejection with grace. Don't bad mouth the company or the interviewers (especially on your social media). Dust yourself off and keep going.

CHAPTER 14

Go Forth and Prosper!

Congratulations! You did it. You have successfully taken the key steps to take control of your career. Even if you decide to move at a slower pace, you are still light years ahead of other people who know they want a change but aren't doing anything to make it happen.

The best thing you can do for yourself is to keep going! Don't lose momentum. Don't lose steam.

We tend to get into cycles where we work hard for a bit and then slip back into complacency. But this is what separates folks who find success from those who stay in unwanted situations. I can also say from experience that I have fallen prey to this mentality, especially in the beginning stages of my coaching business. I had just quit my full-time job, and I was so ready to go and put in weeks' worth of work into the business, then I would stop for a few weeks or a month or so before getting back at it. A lot of that was because I didn't realize how burnt out I was, and my mind was not in the right place.

So lucky for you, you've already done the work of shifting your mindset, assessing if you're burnt out or not, and have taken steps to move forward. I'm proud of you and super excited for what's to come in your career and personal life.

Make sure that you take the time to review this book as necessary. Go back through and repeat any steps that you need or that you tend to have more trouble with or that you may find a little more challenging. The best thing about this book is that you can always rinse and repeat no matter what you're doing. So let's say you get a promotion this time, you know the exact steps to take to get that next promotion or to change careers if that's your next step. Continue to exercise these new muscles and skills so that you're always ready to pivot.

Continue to affirm yourself and switch out affirmations as you have built the self-confidence around them and replace them with new ones that are toward whatever needs you have. Don't throw those old affirmations away because sometimes things creep back up and we just need a nice little reminder of who we are and what we're capable of.

Make sure that you're connecting with companies that are of interest to you and the people within them that can help you within your career or give you more insight. Even if you aren't making a move now and you plan one day to apply to a certain company, build those relationships and put in that leg work now so that when you decide to make that move, you are already ahead of the game.

Be sure to continue to grow your skill sets and knowledge to be of more value as you continue to grow. Remember that knowledge isn't power, but *applied* **knowledge is power**. Don't read this book and then not do anything with it. Use the tools inside here to take advantage of the opportunities ahead. You *can* do this. You are *more than* capable. You are worth it!

If you want more support outside of this book and feel that you need an accountability partner, visit my website and book a FREE 30-minute consultation with me, and make sure to let me know that you bought my book and found it helpful. We can discuss the next steps for our journey together through my different services and brush up on anything that you feel you're still lacking in, and I will be there to cheer you along and celebrate your milestones and all of your success.

I have the option of my 6-week online course that's complimentary to this book with added bonuses for your success, my Facebook group of Career Bosses, as well as different master classes that have been pre-recorded and resume editing services.

I look forward to hearing about your growth and seeing more of us Black professionals thriving and taking over in these spaces. Thank you for taking the time to invest in yourself and trusting me to bring you the knowledge that I feel is not spread enough amongst our community.

Feel free to follow any of my social handles to continue getting tips and tricks for building your professional skills and mindset shift.

You are bomb dot com, and I will see you soon!

> IG: @iamkbepps
> TikTok: @iamkbepps
> LinkedIn: Kaila Epps, MBA, CPC
> YouTube: Kaila Epps
> Services: www.therecruitrefinery.com
> Author site: www.iamkbepps.com
> Online Course: www.bossupyourcareer.com

Feel free to scan the QR code below for quick link access!

ABOUT THE AUTHOR

Kaila Epps, MBA, CPC, aka "Ms. Refine Your Mind," is the Founder and Chief Talent Development Officer of The Recruit Refinery LLC, a career coaching firm empowering black millennial working professionals to turn their professional skills into assets so that they can BOSS UP and take control of a career they love.

She's spent her career in HR business partner and customer service roles at various nonprofits, Fortune 500, and startup companies. She has years of experience conducting interviews, building/editing resumes and cover letters, recruiting candidates, helping professionals define their brand and passions, networking, and speaking publicly.

She's helped her clients get into top 20 MBA programs, pivot into new businesses and build out their brand and value proposition, book paid speaking engagements with various organizations, get hired into general management roles, get connected to key stakeholders in their industry to propel their careers and businesses, and much more.

Kaila is the author of "5 Quick Steps to Go Super Saiyan as an Entrepreneur" and has spoken for multiple organizations around professional development, utilizing one's personal brand to influence their career, the road to entrepreneurship, women's empowerment, and more. She is a proud member of prestigious organizations that are for the empowerment and equality of black (and brown) professionals, such as For(bes) the Culture, Urban League of Greater Atlanta Young Professionals, Sigma Gamma Rho Sorority, Inc., and the Consortium for Graduate Study in Management.

Kaila is passionate about self-development and the development of others. She obtained her MBA from one of the top programs in the U.S. - Indiana University's Kelley School of Business and received her professional coaching certification from an International Coaching Federation accredited program. Kaila enjoys traveling (she's visited 21 countries with a goal to hit 50 countries by 40), watching anime, aerial fitness, and cooking various styles of cuisine with a vegan twist.